SOUVENIR HISTORY OF KNOXVILLE TENNESSEE

The Marble City

and

Great Southern Jobbing Market

Its Importance as a
Manufacturing Center
and its
Manufacturing Possibilities

A REPRODUCTION OF A BOOKLET
ORIGINALLY PUBLISHED AROUND 1907

FROM A COPY OWNED AND GENEROUSLY PROVIDED BY:
ROBERT MCGINNIS

THIS VERSION BY:
BILLIE R. MCNAMARA & CHARLES A. REEVES, JR.
OCT. 2001, WITH MINOR EDITORIAL CHANGES FEB. 2008

©2000, 2001, 2002, 2008
BILLIE R. MCNAMARA
CHARLES A. REEVES, JR.

PRODUCED BY:

Charles A. Reeves, Jr.
Technical Illustration & Publishing
Specializing in Cartography and Genealogy

10812 Dineen Drive (865) 966-5768
Knoxville, Tennessee 37934-1809
e-mail: reevesca@tds.net
Home Page: http://www.ReevesMaps.com

ISBN 978-0-9800984-2-6

How this booklet was produced: Robert McGinnis' original copy was scanned at 600 dpi and the images edited in Adobe Photoshop to remove artifacts. The original was 10" wide by 13" tall, but with wide margins. Although the page size of this copy is somewhat smaller than the original, by reducing the margins the images themselves are only slightly smaller.

Note: Individual prints can be made from the images in this booklet. Contact Charles Reeves for further information (preferably by e-mail).

About the cover: The image is from an old post card, entitled "Knoxville in 1793, cor. Gay and Main Streets." As noted on Page 1 of this booklet, it is from a painting by Lloyd Brasson. That reference indicates the block house was erected in 1786, on the site now occupied by the Court House (the old Knoxville Court House is at Gay and Main).

Table of Contents

Knoxville - Founded in 1792 - Its Early History Progress Prior to the War Between the States — 1

East Tennessee - Natural Resources, Climate, Scenery, Etc.... — 8

Knoxville in 1907 - Growth of the City in the Past Twenty Years — 14

Knoxville as a Manufacturing Center - Resources and Manufacturing Possibilities — 21

Knoxville - The Great Southern Jobbing Market — 27

The [Cherokee] Country Club — 31

Knoxville - As an Educational Center — 33

Knoxville's Banks — 38

The Knoxville Board of Trade — 39
    Some Things the Board of Trade is Trying to Do   42

Manufacturers and Producers Association — 43

The Commercial Club of Knoxville — 44

Real Estate — 48

Advertisements — 49-94

Illustrations

Arnstein Building	15
Baker-Himmel, A boarding School for Boys	36
Beef Cattle on Farm Near Knoxville	9
Block-House Erected in 1786...	1
William Blount	2
William Blount Home	2
Grave of William Blount, Knoxville	2
Historic Daniel Boone Tree	3
Old County Bridge Across Tennessee River	6
View of a Newly Paved Street, Showing Residence of Mr. Daniel Briscoe	19
Melrose Place, One of the Newly Paved Districts, Showing Home of Mr. Ernest Briscoe	19
Brookside Cotton Mills	21
Wm. G. (Parson) Brownlow	5
Modern Concrete and Steel Frame Office Buildings	15
First Capitol of Tennessee	7
Old Catholic Church, Knoxville...1876	7
William F. Chamberlain	44
D. C. Chapman	42
Front View [Cherokee Country Club]	31
Section of Grill Room [Cherokee Country Club]	31
River View from Rear Porch [Cherokee Country Club]	31
A Corner of the Parlor [Cherokee Country Club]	31
The Golf Links [Cherokee Country Club]	31
Knoxville Churches	45
Circle Park, Beautiful Residence Section of Knoxville	20
Water Power, Ducktown Copper Region	11
Opening Mine in Ducktown Copper Region	11
Cumberland Club	16
Admiral Farragut	5
Old East Tennessee Female Institute, Knoxville	6
Elks House, Knoxville	29
First House Erected on the Site of Knoxville	2
Flour Mills	22
Gay Street	27
Gay Street Looking North	14
Gay Street Looking South	14
H. W. Hall	42
Knoxville Homes	32
Island Home Farm Near Knoxville	v
Jersey Cattle on an East Tennessee Farm	9
"The Knobs of East Tennessee"	13
Major-General Henry Knox	3
A Knoxville Brick Plant	25
Knoxville Cotton Mills	22
Knoxville General Hospital	16
Plant of Knoxville Iron Company	21
Knoxville Jobbing Houses	27
Knoxville Post Office	28
View of Knoxville...1876	3
Knoxville Woolen Mills	21
Lincoln Memorial Hospital	16
Logs from East Tennessee Forest on Yard of a Knoxville Lumber Yard	12
Col. Charles McClung	3
Marble Quarry, Near Knoxville	10
Loading Cars with Marble Shipped by Boat from Quarries on Tennessee River	10
James Maynard	43
Road in East Tennessee Mountains	13
George W. Murphy	46
Plant of the Wm. J. Oliver Manufacturing Company	23
Residence of Dr. James Park	4
Views of Residence Streets, Knoxville	18
Pilgrim Congregational Church	16
A Pine Forest in East Tennessee	13
Riverside Woolen Mills	22
Knoxville Public School Buildings	37
W. J. Savage	43
John Sevier	4
Home of John Sevier	4
John Sevier Monument	4
Cary F. Spence	39
Crest of the Unakas [Smoky Mountains]	12
Tannic Acid Factory	23
Oscar M. Tate	43
Along the Beautiful Tennessee	17
Landing on Tennessee River, Knoxville	9
View of Tennessee River from County Bridge, Knoxville	8
View of Tennessee River from Circle Park	11
Views on Tennessee and French Broad Rivers	30
Tennessee River Near University of Tennessee	35
University of Tennessee...1876	7
Dress Parade, University of Tennessee	38
View of University of Tennessee and Fort Sanders	5
Entrance to Grounds - University of Tennessee	33
Science Hall, University of Tennessee	34
University of Tennessee from Tennessee River	34
Driveway at the University of Tennessee	35
Valley View Farms	40, 41
Knoxville's First Water Works	6
Intake, City Water Works	24
West Main Avenue, Bitulithic Paving	28
Central Y.M.C.A. Building	36

ISLAND HOME FARM, NEAR KNOXVILLE

KNOXVILLE

Founded in 1791   Its Early History
Progress Prior to the War
Between the States.

BLOCK-HOUSE ERECTED IN 1786 ON SITE NOW OCCUPIED BY COURT HOUSE
(Photograph from painting by Lloyd Branson)

GOING back a hundred and twenty-one years, we find that the germ of a great city was formed by the erection of a log cabin in a primeval forest on the borderland of the Indian country. This was the first habitation of the white man on the site of Knoxville, built soon after William Blount, of North Carolina, received his appointment from President Washington as governor of the territory South of the Ohio River.

A long time, as man counts it, that hundred and twenty-one years, and full of the stirring events which made history in North America. Volumes could be written on the privations and struggles of the early settlers, the incursions of the Indians, the treaties made and broken, the assaults of savages in great numbers that were checked by a few intrepid whites, the founding of a town in a wilderness, the influx of offshoots from strong and hardy races that carried the course of empire westward from the States of Virginia and North Carolina, the eminence attained by pioneers and their favored sons in the pursuits of peace and on the fields of battle from the Old Dominion to the land of the Montezumas.

It would be interesting to review such history in detail,

but it is beyond the scope of this work. It is the aim of the writer to review briefly the current events, taking special care to present the most important facts.

Knoxville was founded by Col. James White in 1791, and named in honor of Major-General Henry Knox, then Secretary of War.

WILLIAM BLOUNT

The history of the city properly begins, however, with a fort erected by Colonel White after he had entered a large part of this territory as payment for his services in the Revolutionary War. This was in 1786. From that time until the fall of 1793, the history of Indian troubles experienced in the older settlements was repeated here. The first Government troops were stationed in Knoxville during that year, but after Indian hostilities had ceased as a result of very determined voluntary action on the part of the settlers. These settlers came from Virginia and North Carolina and made their homes in and near the town, which became the first seat of Territorial Government, the first Assembly meeting in Knoxville on the fourth Monday of February, 1794.

In 1791 a treaty was made with the Cherokee Indians

FIRST HOUSE ERECTED ON THE SITE OF KNOXVILLE
Built by Col. James White

by Governor Blount. Their principal chiefs and hundreds of their warriors met on the Holston River, and in consideration of an annuity of $1,500 surrendered claims to various tracts of land. This treaty, and one previously made with the Creek Indians, extinguished the Indian title to all lands in this part of the State.

Knoxville was laid off in 1792, the survey and division into lots being made by Col. Charles McClung, probably under direction of Col. White, who owned the land. There never was any public sale of lots. The original owner sold a lot for eight dollars to anyone who would improve and settle on it, and in this way they were disposed of. The town and county soon increased in population

WILLIAM BLOUNT HOME
(Photograph by J. E. Thompson)

sufficiently to protect itself from the incursions of the Indians. Farms were cultivated in the rich valleys, small mills were established and Knoxville became a trading center for quite a large territory. At the second session of the Territorial Assembly a charter was granted for Blount College, which continued in existence until 1807, when it was succeeded by the East Tennessee College, now the University of

GRAVE OF WILLIAM BLOUNT, KNOXVILLE
(Photograph by J. E. Thompson)

Tennessee. William Blount, James White, John Sevier and Davy Crockett were among the prominent men who made Knoxville their home in the early days of its history.

In July, 1795, a road was opened from Knoxville to Nashville so far as to allow the passage of a loaded wagon. About the same time two wagons arrived at Knoxville from South Carolina. The Knoxville trade territory was expand-

HISTORIC DANIEL BOONE TREE
On Which the Famous Pioneer Carved His Name in 1760

COL. CHARLES McCLUNG
Born at Lancaster, Pa., May 19, 1761. Died at Harrodsburg, Ky., in 1835

ing. On the 11th of January, 1796, a convention met here for the purpose of forming a State Constitution, and on the 1st of June following Tennessee was admitted into the Union. Knoxville, by a provision of the State Constitution, was the seat of government until 1802. Subsequent legislatures kept it here until 1817.

Steamboat navigation was introduced on the Tennessee River in 1826. The East Tennessee and Georgia Railroad was completed in 1855, and soon afterward business received new impetus by the building of the East Tennessee and Virginia road to this place.

MAJOR-GENERAL HENRY KNOX

VIEW OF KNOXVILLE
From Photograph Taken About 1876

In 1826 a systematic effort was made for the first time to improve the streets of Knoxville. The citizens elected their first mayor in 1839, W. B. A. Ramsey receiving forty-nine votes to forty-eight cast for James Park. In 1860 the Knoxville and Kentucky Railroad, now the Knoxville and

JOHN SEVIER

RESIDENCE OF DR. JAMES PARK,
KNOXVILLE
This House was Planned and First Bricks Laid by John Sevier

Ohio branch of the Southern, had been completed as far as Clinton, Tenn.

Before the day of the railroads there was considerable progress made in the construction of public highways in East Tennessee. The first road was surveyed by Charles McClung in 1792, from Knoxville west to Campbell's Station and thence to the western boundary of Knox County. Thus we see that the good roads movement in this county was coeval with the founding of the city. The highway referred to followed along the ridges pretty closely after an Indian trail as far as Sinking Creek. The road as originally

line of stages was operated prior to 1850, called the "Great Western Line," running from Raleigh, N. C., where connection was made with rail and steamboat to Washington, westward by way of Greensboro, Salisbury, Rutherfordton, Asheville and Warm Springs to Knoxville, a distance of 385 miles. The time between this city and Washington was advertised as "six days and six hours," and the fare was forty-four dollars. The journey is now made over the same route in less than twenty-four hours. Since the war pike building has been carried on as an important part of the work of the county, there being at this time over one hundred miles of good macadamized roads leading out of Knoxville.

With early road building and improved river transportation came the development of Knoxville as a jobbing

HOME OF JOHN SEVIER
Knoxville

JOHN SEVIER MONUMENT
On Site of First Block House

laid out by Mr. McClung was cut most of the way through the primeval forest. It was about thirty feet wide, the width being extended to fifty feet many years later, and formed a part of the national highway from Washington to Knoxville, Nashville, Montgomery and New Orleans. Over this road a

center. It was a good market, supplying a territory embracing portions of several Southern States, before railroads were built in this section. Two of the five inhabitants of Knoxville, when it was laid out in 1792—Samuel and Nathaniel Cowan—opened a general store here. They were followed by Hugh Dunlap, Humes Fryar and others, bartering for deer, bear and coon skins, farm produce, etc., forming the principal trading operations. Goods were brought to Knoxville in wagons and boats, and distributed in the same way during the early days of wholesaling. In 1820 James H. Cowan, a nephew of the first merchants of the place, opened a store here, and later formed a partnership with Hugh M. White. In 1832 Mr. Cowan entered into partnership with Mr. Perez Dickenson. Out of this firm grew the wholesale house of Cowan, McClung & Co., which is described in the advertising section of this book as one of the leading establishments of our present great jobbing market.

WM. G. (PARSON) BROWNLOW
His Residence and Editorial Rooms

ADMIRAL FARRAGUT
Born at Lowe's Ferry, Near Knoxville Where Monument Has Been Erected

VIEW OF UNIVERSITY OF TENNESSEE AND FORT SANDERS
From Photograph Taken Soon After the Close of the War

The first exclusive wholesale house in Knoxville was that of McClung, Wallace & Co., established in 1837. Goods were sold by this house in East Tennessee, North Georgia and Northern Alabama. Knoxville has been a jobbing market for nearly three-quarters of a century.

OLD COUNTY BRIDGE ACROSS TENNESSEE RIVER
Torn Down and Replaced by Steel Bridge in 1898

KNOXVILLE'S FIRST WATER WORKS
Water Hauled from Springs by "Uncle" Richard Sneed and Sold to People in the City

OLD EAST TENNESSEE FEMALE INSTITUTE, KNOXVILLE
Where the Mothers of Many of Knoxville's Leading Business Men Were Educated.—From Photograph Taken Many Years Ago

UNIVERSITY OF TENNESSEE
Photograph Taken About 1876

FIRST CAPITOL OF TENNESSEE
Building Still Standing on State Street, Knoxville

OLD CATHOLIC CHURCH, KNOXVILLE
From Photograph Taken in 1876

EAST TENNESSEE

Natural Resources, Climate, Scenery, Etc., of a Great Favored Region of the South of Which Knoxville is the Industrial and Commercial Center

IT has been said that if East Tennessee was walled in so completely as to render communication with the rest of the world impossible, its people would still have everything necessary to the permanent comfort and happiness of man.

The natural resources of this section are so great and varied, and the problem of living—even of living well and making money besides—so easy of solution, that it was practically shut in by a wall of indifference for many generations. Prosperous business men are now living in its metropolis—men who have passed more than half a century in the successful pursuit of wealth—who have never in all of their long lives thought of inviting outside capital to aid in the work of building up their town. Why should they? Exploiting resources was not a part of their business. Such work would not have been considered as necessary to their welfare. They made money. The town grew in spite of the old spirit of conservatism. If people came with money to invest, or with a willingness to engage in some useful occupation, they met with a hearty welcome—but they were not invited. They were generally prospectors who stumbled upon the rich leads of this city and section by accident.

The work of development that went forward by slow stages for many years finally led to an industrial awakening that is making this region famous. Enough has been done to give some idea of the extent and value of our resources, and to prove conclusively that success in many fields of occupation is easier of attainment here than anywhere else in the land.

In East Tennessee are found fertile soils, pure water

VIEW OF TENNESSEE RIVER FROM COUNTY BRIDGE, KNOXVILLE

and a delightful climate. The man who wishes to engage in general farming, stock or poultry raising is offered here the very best locations in the South. In no part of this favored region would he be far removed from good markets. In many places he would have the advantages of railroads and excellent pikes. Clover and the grasses flourish here. Corn, wheat and oats are profitable crops. Truck farming and fruit growing are industries that pay. The man of small means will find here many opportunities to engage in paying enterprises. The small farm, factory, quarry or mine will yield large returns on investments under efficient management. Abundant proof of this is shown on every hand. The visitor who goes into the manufacturing districts of Knoxville will conclude that it is destined to become a city of small factories, as there are so many new enterprises here that may be properly classed under that head; but when he learns that most of the large concerns started in business on a scale quite as unpretentious and attained to their present importance in a few years through rapid and steady growth, he will have a better view of the trend of development.

The possibilities of farming, mining and other industries in East Tennessee are far greater than evidences of progress indicate. There is great room for improvement and expansion. The specialist, the man of intelligence and enterprise, can work wonders here.

To name in itemized detail the natural resources of

BEEF CATTLE ON FARM NEAR KNOXVILLE

JERSEY CATTLE ON AN EAST TENNESSEE FARM

East Tennessee that are susceptible of development for the use of man, would be in a large measure to catalogue the natural products of the animal, vegetable and mineral kingdoms to be found in the temperate zone of America. This is no idle boast, but a fact easily demonstrated and as easily explained. The geological forces that uplifted the towering walls of the great Unakas and laid down the deep valleys, brought to the surface a variety of rich structure ranging in unbroken succession from the oldest Archaean down through the carboniferous. Thus was furnished the building material for every variety of soil. At the same time the other controlling factor in vegetation, climate, was extended through several degrees of temperature by difference in altitude from 800 feet above the sea in the valleys to more than 5,000 feet on the crests of the Unakas. As the outgrowth of the combination of endless variety of soil and wide range of temperature there may be grown in East Tennessee almost every plant found from Florida to Canada. Sugar cane and rice are about the only staple crops of

America that cannot be grown with profit. While the soil is generous and friendly, the climate is of that peculiar character that stimulates without enervating; neither so cold as to benumb the energies, nor so hot as to relax the physical system. In these two chief factors in agricultural wealth, climate and soil, East Tennessee challenges comparison with all America. Among industrial resources these are first considered because history teaches that they lie at the foundation of all independent and permanent prosperity. However rich in mineral resources a country may be, its people can never be independent or, in the mass, prosperous if it does not produce food enough to feed its people. In this particular the wealth of East Tennessee is happily balanced. While she has packed away in her mountains minerals to employ millions of miners, she has the soil and climate to feed them most bountifully.

Next in importance in the industrial resources to be named are the facilities for making up the raw materials, for smelting the iron and manufacturing the lumber, clays and stones. California, with all of her wealth of gold and tropical luxuriance of vegetation, is tremendously handi-

LANDING ON TENNESSEE RIVER, KNOXVILLE

MARBLE QUARRY, NEAR KNOXVILLE

capped by the scarcity of her water power and the entire absence of coal. Owing to these natural defects she can never become a manufacturing region. East Tennessee presents the strongest possible contrast to California in this respect in the number and volume of her water courses, the extent and high quality of her beds of iron ore, and fields of coal, surmounted by forests of timber. The art of man could not plan these great elemental forces of industry more conveniently than nature has placed them. Today it is practicable to stand at the mouth of a number of coal mines

LOADING CARS WITH MARBLE SHIPPED BY BOAT FROM QUARRIES ON TENNESSEE RIVER

WATER POWER, DUCKTOWN COPPER REGION

and throw a stone across a ravine through which runs an everlasting stream of water on to an iron bank, the bed of the stream being limestone. Thus literally within a stone's throw nature has collected all the essentials for the making of iron. While this is true of many favored spots, in no part of East Tennessee are the iron banks and coal beds separated by a hundred miles.

The water courses that have carved out the great valley and its numerous tributary valleys all converge to form the Tennessee River into one great common channel of transportation for the whole region of East Tennessee. Thus by its close combination of all of the great elements of industrial prosperity, it may be not inappropriately claimed that East Tennessee furnishes a striking practical illustration of our national motto—E Pluribus Unum—many in one.

Geographical position is not less important to the industrial prosperity of a city, section or State than street location to the commercial success of a merchant. So good stands and corner lots have their extra value emphasized in higher rents. So a city, section or State may claim among its valuable industrial resources a favorable position in relation to the great markets of the country of which they form a part. Tennessee has been well described as "the pivot plate on which turns the interstate commerce of the North and South, with Knoxville, Nashville and Memphis as its three receiving and distributing foci." East Tennessee, an intermediate position between the North and South, is in position to take advantage of the markets of both. For example, in the poultry business, which has grown to such large proportions, the trade goes North in winter and South in summer. This is but one example of a general law oper-

OPENING MINE IN DUCKTOWN COPPER REGION

ating in many lines of business, and illustrating the commercial value of East Tennessee's geographical position.

The number and variety of the mineral springs in East Tennessee are literally numberless. Many of them have long established reputations as health resorts and the waters of two of them are to be found on sale at almost every soda water fount in the land—a never failing source of wealth.

Of the marbles and other famous building stones it is needless to speak; their reputation has gone abroad over all the land. It is not so well known, however, that the building clays and potting clays of East Tennessee are as rich in variety and beauty as its marbles and even more abundant. But few persons know that the exquisite Rookwood ware, which has made Cincinnati famous, is all made from East Tennessee clays, but such we believe to be the case.

The area of East Tennessee is 13,112 square miles, or more territory than either Maryland, Vermont or New Hampshire, and nearly as much as Massachusetts, Connecti-

VIEW OF TENNESSEE RIVER FROM CIRCLE PARK

cut and Rhode Island combined. The general formation consists primarily of two great mountain walls, two thousand to six thousand feet above sea level, enclosing an immense valley one hundred and seventy-five miles long by thirty-four to fifty miles wide. This valley, known as the Great Valley of East Tennessee, is itself a series of minor valleys, separated one from another by long parallel ridges and broken hills, many of them several hundred feet high.

Scenery, Waterways, Etc.

Countries with high, heavily timbered mountains, wooded hills, broad fertile valleys, and winding rivers, always afford the finest landscape pictures. The scenery of East Tennessee is not surpassed by any in the world. In never-ending magnificence it greets the eye at every turn. This section is often and aptly called the "Switzerland of America." Its mountains, while lacking the dizzy heights of the Alps and the rugged massiveness of the Rockies, possess a symmetry of form and outline which, harmonizing with sky and field and forest and purple atmosphere, presents picture after picture which captivate all beholders.

The whole of East Tennessee is drained by the Tennessee, one of the longest and most important of American rivers, and by its numerous tributaries—the Holston, French Broad, Pigeon, Little Tennessee, Hiwassee, Emory, Powell and the Clinch, as well as numerous smaller streams. All these streams furnish abundant water power sites for manufacturing purposes.

CREST OF THE UNAKAS
5000 Feet Above the Sea

Knoxville and East Tennessee possess an almost ideal climate for comfort and health, the combined effect of its

LOGS FROM EAST TENNESSEE FORESTS ON YARD OF A KNOXVILLE LUMBER COMPANY

ROAD IN EAST TENNESSEE MOUNTAINS

latitude, altitude and excellent drainage. Miasmatic diseases, cyclones, sun-strokes, and pestilence are unknown.

Forest Resources

There are 135 species of trees in this section of the State growing on its more than five million acres of timber lands. Those of the greatest commercial value are the pines, of which the most valuable are the varieties known as the "short-leaf" and the "white pine." The short-leaf is the second most valuable of the Southern hardwood pines, standing next to the "long-leaf," growing in States further South. There are thousands of acres of white pine in East Tennessee that will yield from five to fifty thousand and even one hundred thousand feet per acre. There are vast growths of black spruce, balsams and firs. Then there is the maple, the ash, the holly, and the sweet and yellow birch which grow to enormous size. The chestnut, red and white oaks, the black cherry and the sugar maple, all magnificent growths. Huge poplar trees of centuries of growth cover the coves and mountain sides with their gigantic forms. The well known beech is found everywhere. The yellow buckeye is unsurpassed as to its size. The cucumber magnolia, an excellent timber, is plentiful. So are the yellow locust, and the white-leaved basswood—both so valuable. Big chestnut timber is abundant, so also are the various kinds of hickory, walnut, cedar, elm and gum.

At present more attention is being turned to developing our vast timber resources than ever before. Companies largely capitalized have built railroads into the mountains, established large plants and are turning out millions of feet of lumber from poplar, oak, pine, cherry, walnut, chestnut, locust, elm and other species of trees found in commercial quantities.

At a glance we see that the natural resources of East Tennessee embrace the wealth of air, earth and water. The rocks and soils that make the framework of the earth, the plants that spring from it, the animals that live upon it, the minerals and precious metals that are dug out of it, and the waters under the earth—each manifold in kind and rich in quality. Nature has done all for East Tennessee that the heart of reasonable man could desire.

"THE KNOBS O' TENNESSEE"

A PINE FOREST IN EAST TENNESSEE

KNOXVILLE IN 1907

Growth of the City in the Past Twenty Years

ABOUT the time that the eyes of Northern capitalists were first turned to the New South, the old city of Knoxville began to show signs of an awakening. Its growth since 1887 has been steady and healthful. Its population in 1890 was 22,500; at the present time it is over 85,000. Its small manufacturing business of two decades ago has increased until it can show manufactured products amounting to more than $20,000,000 a year. Its streets at that time were little better than macadamized roads; today it has many miles of streets paved with asphalt and brick, and the work of paving is going on at a rapid rate in many parts of the city. In a short time Knoxville will have the best modern streets and sidewalks, and more of them, than any city of its size in the country. Twenty years ago Knoxville had no electric railways. Today the city has forty miles of the heaviest track in the South, running to all parts of the city and suburbs, and has an electric car service second to none. Knoxville is one of the best lighted cities in the United States. Its water supply is all that could be desired—the purest water to be found in the country, and plenty of it for all purposes. Here are some facts and figures which will be of interest to investors:

GAY STREET LOOKING NORTH

Knoxville does a jobbing business of about $50,000,000 annually.

Knoxville has nine banks, the deposits of which amount to $12,000,000; the annual clearings over $75,000,000, more than 300 per cent greater than ten years ago.

Knoxville is the largest hardwood mantel manufacturing point in the world.

Knoxville is the greatest clothing manufacturing point in the Southern States.

Knoxville is situated in the midst of the largest undeveloped hardwood region of the country.

Knoxville has ten educational institutions, including the State University. It has also a fine public school system.

Knoxville has an exceptional record for textile manufacturing.

Knoxville is the headquarters for the coal market of the Southeastern States.

Knoxville has the cheapest steam coal fuel of any city in the South.

Knoxville is the largest city between Nashville, Tenn., and Charleston, S. C., the largest between Cincinnati and Atlanta, the largest between Birmingham and Richmond.

GAY STREET LOOKING SOUTH

ARNSTEIN BUILDING
Fireproof Steel Frame Building

MODERN CONCRETE AND STEEL FRAME OFFICE BUILDINGS

LINCOLN MEMORIAL HOSPITAL

KNOXVILLE GENERAL HOSPITAL

Knoxville is situated 1,000 feet above sea-level in the heart of the Southern Appalachian country, and with the exception of Asheville, N. C., holds the coolest record for summer of all Southern cities.

Knoxville has over one hundred arrivals and departures of passenger trains daily.

Knoxville has a record for increase in wealth of manufacturing between 1900 and 1905 reached by no city in Tennessee, and surpassed by few in the country. The growth was 100 per cent in the five years.

Knoxville's building operations aggregated a million and a half dollars for a year past. This does not include a half million dollars spent in building around the corporate limits.

Knoxville is located in the center of the most extensive railroad building operations of the South.

Knoxville has unlimited water power facilities in the Tennessee, French Broad, Holston, Clinch, and Little Tennessee rivers.

Knoxville has direct, short-line railroad routes to all important points of the country.

Knoxville has seventy woodworking establishments.

Knoxville manufactures about 300 kinds of products.

Knoxville has a $75,000.00 Y. M. C. A. building and many handsome churches.

Knoxville is represented by about 600 drummers in its trade territory.

Knoxville has four good hotels and needs more.

Knoxville has more handsome apartment houses than any city of its size in the South.

Knoxville is located on the deposit of the famous Tennessee marble.

Knoxville has two railway systems—the Southern and Louisville and Nashville, with their many branches.

CUMBERLAND CLUB

PILGRIM CONGREGATIONAL CHURCH

(Photos by J. E. Thompson)

ALONG THE BEAUTIFUL TENNESSEE
(Photos by J. E. Thompson)

VIEWS OF RESIDENCE STREETS, KNOXVILLE
Showing New Bitulithic and Asphalt Paving

(Photos by J. E. Thompson)

VIEW OF A NEWLY PAVED STREET, SHOWING RESIDENCE OF MR. DANIEL BRISCOE

MELROSE PLACE, ONE OF THE NEWLY PAVED DISTRICTS, SHOWING HOME OF MR. EARNEST BRISCOE

Photos by J. E. Thompson

Knoxville is the geographical center of the Southern Railway System, and on a line drawn from New York to New Orleans.

Knoxville's vegetable and fruit market, supplied from fertile farms, gardens and orchards of East Tennessee, is the wonder of visitors.

Knoxville is an important manufacturer of iron. It is situated near important iron ore deposits.

Knoxville's tax rate is fixed by the charter at $1.25.

Knoxville has six commercial organizations.

The Board of Trade is an organization composed of Knoxville's leading financial and business citizens, with a membership of something over five hundred, enthusiastically at work to advance the interests of this city.

The Commercial Club is a similar organization that devotes itself particularly to advancing the jobbing interests of the city and has a large membership.

The Manufacturers' and Producers' Association, as its

CIRCLE PARK; BEAUTIFUL RESIDENCE SECTION OF KNOXVILLE
(Photo by J. E. Thompson)

Knoxville has a public library of twenty thousand volumes, is endowed and free.

Knoxville is a saloonless city.

Knoxville has two daily newspapers—the Journal and Tribune, morning, Republican; the Knoxville Sentinel, evening, Democrat. It also issues The Business Magazine, the Industrious Hen, the Knoxville Independent (labor), the University Record, of the University of Tennessee; the Methodist-Advocate Journal, and the Holston Christian Advocate.

name implies, is organized to advance chiefly the interests of Knoxville's manufacturers.

The Retail Merchants' Association has a large membership and is doing good work in the interests of local dealers.

The Travelers' Protective Association, composed of drummers, has one thousand members.

The United Commercial Travelers is an organization composed of traveling men who represent Knoxville's wholesale and jobbing houses.

KNOXVILLE AS A MANUFACTURING CENTER

Resources and Manufacturing Possibilities

KNOXVILLE presents extraordinary advantages to the manufacturer. It can be proven in many ways, but probably nothing is more convincing than the figures given by the Government Census Bureau showing the growth in manufactured output. For the period between 1900 and 1905 this reliable authority reveals that Knoxville has grown 100.5 per cent.

All of the elements that make for success in manufacturing are found in Knoxville and tributary to it. The only thing lacking is the application of capital and skill.

The Raw Materials

What are these advantages? As shown in the article on the Resources of East Tennessee, raw material of a hundred kinds is near at hand.

Thirteen varieties of timber in great abundance, awaiting to be manufactured into thousands of articles.

Iron ore of various kinds and in greater abundance than in any similar area in the South, sleeps in valley and mountain side of the Southern Appalachian country. Its rare manganese ore is drawn upon from far and near; its rich brown ores pour in long trains into the furnace district. Yet it is only barely touched.

Marble—the most beautiful in the world—acknowledged by sculptors to have the rarest tints and finest quality of all marbles, a favorite for inside decoration and for monuments, as durable as granite, unlimited in supply, skirts the borders of Knoxville and affords employment for a great number of men, but which shows only a beginning in the way of development.

Clay in great varieties and tints, suitable for the manufacture of common and fancy brick, and pottery of various kinds, now being successfully utilized, yet abounds in every community and is inexhaustible.

Cement rock, thus far manufactured to only a limited

KNOXVILLE WOOLEN MILLS   BROOKSIDE COTTON MILLS   PLANT OF KNOXVILLE IRON COMPANY

extent, is found in great abundance in the region of Knoxville. This and other lime rock is now being converted into lime, macadam and building stone.

Knoxville is situated not far from the famous Ducktown copper region, in which is located one of the largest plants of the country. Evidences have been found that this copper deposit extends northward many miles and in the future will be still more extensively developed.

Knoxville is built on a zinc deposit. The ore exists in varying quantities on two sides of it. A problem of separation from the dolomite exists which is being gradually solved by Northern capital, which has been experimenting at great cost trying to perfect a process of separation. Once solved, Knoxville will surpass Joplin, Missouri, as a zinc center.

is presented. Fruits of every variety grown in the South thrive here, many valuable ones growing wild. Live stock finds no more congenial place to thrive. Grains grow luxuriantly on alluvial and rich uplands. Vegetables of every variety are grown successfully.

So much for the raw material.

When we turn to consider the cost of manufacturing, aside from the cheap raw material at hand, the prospects grow more and more inviting.

The cost of power is an item of expense which a manufacturer must consider carefully in locating his plant. What has Knoxville to offer as an advantage in this respect? A very exceptional one. It offers the cheapest and best steam fuel of the South from the coal mines a few miles away.

FLOUR MILLS   RIVERSIDE WOOLEN MILLS   KNOXVILLE COTTON MILLS

Knoxville is situated on the border of the greatest undeveloped coal area in the United States. It is the headquarters of seventy-five coal operators, who supply the larger part of the coal sold in North Carolina, South Carolina, Georgia, Tennessee, Eastern Kentucky, while coal is sold to some extent in Florida, Ohio and Illinois.

Other mineral resources of the region tributary to Knoxville and developed to only a limited extent, when they might be more fully, are barytes, slate, corundrum, lead, gold and iron pyrites.

Turning to the possibilities of manufacturing articles of food from the products of the farm, an inviting prospect

Some of Knoxville's big plants are burning steam coal that costs them $1.10 per ton at the plant. When it comes to paying $2.50, $3.00 to $4.00 per ton for coal, as some manufacturers do in many places where long hauls make the freight bills large, Knoxville's advantage in this respect may be seen.

But Knoxville is doubly blessed in this respect, because it not only has cheap steam coal, but vast possibilities of cheap water power. The great Southern Appalachian country drains toward Knoxville, and all the rivers present almost infinite possibilities of water power. Two notable enterprises for this purpose are now under way.

PLANT OF THE WM. J. OLIVER MANUFACTURING COMPANY

TANNIC ACID FACTORY

What of the labor supply? This is another important question of the manufacturer. It can be answered by saying that Knoxville does not have labor shortages. The natives of the valleys, hills and mountains of East Tennessee, Southeastern Kentucky, Southwestern Virginia, Western North Carolina, and North Georgia are the most prolific in progeny, as the census shows, in the United States. Thus far an unfailing stream of competent and satisfactory labor has poured into Knoxville from this region round about.

What of the cost of living?—a question which has its bearing on wages. The answer that Knoxville is able to make—thanks to fertile farms, orchards and gardens, with all their great variety of products surrounding Knoxville—is that the cost of living from the food standpoint is lower raw material and for sending the manufactured products away to market by the shortest hauls.

But in addition to the railroads is the navigable Tennessee River flowing through it, now used to some extent, but certain to be a great highway of commerce into the heart of the Mississippi Valley when important river improvements are completed.

What of the climate? It is the happiest all the year round medium in all the wide country. Situated as it is 1,000 feet above sea level, surrounded by loftier altitudes, with great mountains east and west, a summer weather never as hot as Chicago, Detroit, New York and other Northern cities, while winter is cold enough to make one feel good, Knoxville recognizes no superior climate. Think

INTAKE, CITY WATER WORKS

than any city of its size in the South, if not in the whole country. Because Knoxville is a large manufacturing center for clothing from the wool and cotton to the suit, Knoxville gets cheap clothing. Rents are reasonable. It can, therefore, be justly claimed that the cost of living is exceptionally low in Knoxville.

What of transportation facilities? Glance at a railroad map and see how railroads run in every direction out of Knoxville direct to the great marts of the nation. Note, too, how the railroads built for developing the resources of the Southern Appalachian country follow the courses of the streams and converge upon Knoxville, the geographical and commercial center. Thus may it be seen that Knoxville is well supplied with railroad facilities, both for securing of the saving of fuel and clothing to the laboring class afforded by such weather and its bearing on wages!

Some other advantages in brief are streams on which to build plants and draw a free water supply, a big jobbing business, and wide established reputation, absence of coal famines, a reasonable tax rate, a liberal city and State policy toward manufacturers, the absence of the saloon and its demoralizing effects on labor, exceptional educational advantages for the children of manufacturers, a cordial hospitality toward strangers.

Variety of Products

That Knoxville is situated with wonderful adaptation to a vast variety of manufacturing is evidenced by the fact that it manufactures more than three hundred kinds of articles. The following is a list that doubtless falls short of the actual number of various sorts of products:

Advertising signs (electric).
Awnings.
Aluminum castings.
Bar iron.
Baskets.
Bed springs.
Blank books.
Blueing.
Bottle goods.
Boxes (wooden).
Brick (ornamental).
Brass castings.
Brick cars.
Architectural iron.
Axles.
Balconies (iron).
Barytes.
Bed couches.
Beer.
Blinds.
Boilers.
Boxes (paper).
Brakes.
Brick (building).
Bread.
Brick (vitrified).
Cigars.
Coke.
Collars (men).
Desks.
Elevators.
Electricity.
Engravings.
Excelsior.
Feeds (horse and cattle).
Fertilizers.
Flour mill machinery.
Furniture.
Ginger ale.
Grocers' supplies.
Galvanized iron.
Clothings.
Collars (horse).
Cotton goods.
Doors.
Eczemaline.
Engines (gasoline).
Extracts, flavoring.
Face brick.
Fence (iron).
Flour.
Furnaces.
Grates.
Grate bars.
Gas supplies.
Handles.

A KNOXVILLE BRICK PLANT

Brooms.
Building material.
Building stone.
Corduroys.
Cashmeres.
Candy.
Cars (railroad).
Carving and mouldings.
Castings (iron).
Chairs.
Cement.
Chewing gum.
Building blocks (concrete).
Buggies.
Cotton duck.
Cakes.
Cabinets.
Car wheels.
Carriages.
Caskets and coffins.
Catsup.
Chests (cedar).
Cement sidewalks.
Cider.
Harness.
Hosiery yarns.
Ice.
Iron articles.
Jugs.
Launches.
Lime.
Machinery (conveying and
Mantels.
Marble (commercial).
Millinery.
Mining cars.
Hats.
Hosiery.
Ice cream.
Jeans.
Lathes.
Leather goods.
Lumber.
elevating).
Marble mill machinery.
Mattresses.
Meal (corn).
Models.

Monuments.
Optical goods.
Packing cases.
Patent medicines.
Pavements.
Plaster (wood fiber).
Porch columns.
Post Cards.
Proprietary medicines.
Stamps (rubber).
Saws.
Shirts.
Sash.
Smokestacks.
Surgical instruments.
Soil pipe.
Tannic acid.
Trucks.
Tinware.
Underwear (ladies').
Vinegar.
Vessels (expanding and collapsing).
Veneering.
Newspapers.
Overalls.
Packing house products.
Patterns.
Picture frames.
Pottery.
Photographs.
Powder.
Pulleys.
Saddles.
Shafting.
Skirts.
Shoes.
Stoves.
Suspenders.
Tanks.
Telephone supplies.
Trunks.
Umbrellas.
Underwear (men's).
Velveteens.
Whiskey.

Manufacturing Opportunities

With what has been said and what has been shown as to the variety of products of the manufacturing plants of Knoxville, it may be seen that a wide range of possibilities exist for the man who has the money and the knowledge.

Some of these that appear to the writer as worth emphasizing as being especially attractive are mentioned. Iron and steel in the thousands of different forms for which it is used, will here find all of the sorts of ore needed—the coke, the lime needful for furnaces, with the great market of the South and the West assured for the finished products.

Situated as Knoxville is in the center of the Southern Appalachian belt, the greatest hardwood belt left in the country, this city is well located for the manufacturing and marketing of furniture, cabinets, desks, veneer, handles, wagons, carriages, agricultural implements, and everything for which hard wood is generally used.

Knoxville affords an exceptionally favorable location for the manufacture of marble specialties, mosaic, etc., situated as it is where marble costs little and where it is found in great variety.

The possibilities of the use of the clays that abound in the region, have not yet dawned. A great variety, striking in colors, are capable of being turned to account in numerous ways from brick manufacturing to fancy pottery.

Unquestionably there are many opportunities for the manufacture of Portland cement in this region. None of them have yet been put to use. Knoxville holds out special advantages for the manufacture of leather. It is a large shoe jobbing point and specially well situated with reference to some of the largest tanneries of the country near Knoxville.

Knoxville is the leading clothing manufacturing point in the South. With the advantages it has, there is no reason why it should not be the leading one of the country.

As for textiles, it has taken high rank. The prosperity of the textile manufacturing plants of Knoxville and the character of goods turned out are strong arguments in favor of other such industries.

Many more opportunities are offered. The manufacturer who is seeking a location cannot afford to overlook the advantages which are peculiar to Knoxville as to no other city in the South.

KNOXVILLE

The Great Southern Jobbing Market

FOR more than seventy years Knoxville has been a wholesale market. There were few houses here prior to 1860, but a number of firms embarked in the jobbing business after the war. Nearly every one met with success, which proved two things: that the merchants were qualified and equipped for business, and that Knoxville was geographically situated to command a large trade. About the year 1880 other large houses were opened and a new impetus was

KNOXVILLE JOBBING HOUSES

given to the jobbing business of the city. Today Knoxville sells more shoes than Louisville, Ky. Her large dry goods and notion houses are equal to the average in Cincinnati or Louisville. Her business men pay $220,000 in fire insurance premiums per annum. The capital employed is sufficient to supply foreign and domestic goods in immense quantities and at the very lowest prices. Last year her sales of dry goods and notions amounted to some three millions of dollars! In ready-made clothing, pants, overalls and gents' furnishings, she leads all the cities of the South. Some of her clothing merchants buy their goods in the piece direct from the different mills throughout the country, and manufacture them under their own immediate supervision and direction in New York City, thus affording retailers an opportunity of buying at first hands and saving the cost of the middleman. In this line her trade extends from West

Virginia and Virginia, Kentucky and Tennessee, through the Carolinas, Georgia, Alabama, Mississippi westward to Arkansas and Texas. The different lines of merchandise are better represented in Knoxville than in any other Southern city, and, according to her size, her commerce is larger than that of any other city in the United States. It is estimated that her business last year amounted to the vast sum of fifty millions of dollars! This great volume of trade is due to the well-trained experience and conservative, yet liberal, methods of her merchants; the increasing facilities of transportation, her competing lines of railroad running in every direction, and to her geographical position being in the very center of the circle described by Cincinnati, Louisville, Nashville, Atlanta, Charlotte and Lynchburg. Thus she has decided advantage in proximity to retail merchants and a much lower rate of freight.

Knoxville enjoys the reputation of great liberality to her patrons. Through her splendid Commercial Club she is holding out her open hand of hospitality and cordiality to every merchant who will accept her gracious invitation, to come and get acquainted with our merchants and test the qualities of this market.

GAY STREET

The business men of Knoxville are sending out daily from 40,000 to 50,000 pieces of mail to their customers in the South. Every one of these, whether personal letter or invoice—by its close prices and liberal terms—is an invitation to seek the best that can be had for the money, and come to Knoxville to get it.

The advantages offered here are becoming more widely known each season. Buyers have discovered that the various lines are better represented in Knoxville than in any other Southern market, and that goods carried by Knoxville jobbers are selected to meet the wants of Southern people, which insures good business for the retailers who handle them. Many prominent merchants in Kentucky, Georgia, Alabama and other Southern States, who once thought that "going East" to buy goods was an important part of their business, now save money on transportation and freight rates by coming to Knoxville, and secure better stocks than they could

WEST MAIN AVENUE, BITULITHIC PAVING
(Photo by J. E. Thompson)

select from the lines that are carried for all sections by Eastern firms. And their number is increasing. Knoxville, the great Southern jobbing market, is a greater market this year than it was a year ago, and its growth will continue with the development of the industrial and commercial interests of the Southern States.

The following statements concerning various lines carried by Knoxville houses, will be of interest to buyers:

Clothing

No city in the South does as large a jobbing and wholesale clothing business as Knoxville.

It is possible that Louisville, Kentucky, surpasses Knoxville in the amount of pants manufactured and jobbed, but neither that city nor any other in the South is in the same class as Knoxville in both the manufacture and jobbing of suits and clothing.

It is estimated that the local jobbing business in clothing will aggregate the sum of $3,000,000, in the course of a year. The trade territory is not limited to the South, but, of course, a great part of the goods jobbed from Knoxville is sold in the Southern States. About one hundred traveling men are sent out by the clothing firms of Knoxville to represent them in the trade in the South and West.

Dry Goods and Notions

Knoxville has a business in wholesale dry goods and notions which aggregates several millions of dollars annually.

It has built up this business because of the advantages which it possesses; chiefly its central location in the South, its splendid railroad facilities, its reliable wholesale dry goods firms and the large stocks which are carried.

Four of the largest and best established dry goods and notion houses in the South are located in this city.

Hats

Knoxville's wholesale hat business amounts to about a half million dollars annually, and is growing. Merchants can find here the latest styles and the greatest variety of everything in this line that the diversified trade of the South demands.

Shoes

About three million dollars' worth of shoes are sold annually by Knoxville jobbers. This large shoe business is done in Alabama, Mississippi, Tennessee, Kentucky, Virginia, North Carolina, South Carolina and Georgia. Knoxville has three exclusive shoe jobbing houses and others do both a retail and wholesale business.

Between forty and fifty traveling men represent Knoxville shoe houses in the territory above mentioned. The shoe business of Knoxville has grown up largely in the last ten or fifteen years. It has been won by selling high-class and high-price shoes as well as the cheap varieties, but more particularly the former.

It may be said for the credit of the shoe jobbers of Knoxville that they have been able to stand off all foreign

KNOXVILLE POST OFFICE
(Photo by J. E. Thompson)

competition, and have steadily held to and increased their trade.

Drugs

Over a million dollars' worth of drugs are sold by wholesale firms of Knoxville each year. This is a record that stands in the forefront of the drug business of the South. Moreover, it is growing and spreading in its scope. The entire South is covered by traveling salesmen and in some lines the "medicine man" goes beyond the borders of the South.

The bulk of this business is general drugs and druggists' supplies. Knoxville is not yet in front in the manufacture of patent medicines, but it has some thriving establishments of this kind.

Hardware

Knoxville does the largest jobbing business in hardware and kindred lines of any city east of the Mississippi River. The territory covered by the hardware wholesalers of Knoxville is embraced by seven Southern States, viz.: Tennessee, Kentucky, Virginia, North Carolina, South Carolina, Georgia and Alabama. Traveling men go out from Knoxville over all this territory and visit the trade several times during the year.

Knoxville enjoys many advantages as a wholesale hardware market. In the first place, it is situated in a section of the South that is rapidly building up a trade in hardware and which gives great promise for the future as the natural resources are developed.

In the second place, Knoxville is well situated as to both the receiving of hardware goods from the East and Middle West, where they are largely manufactured, and their distribution to the trade territory. Thus there is a saving of railroad rates.

Confections, Etc.

Knoxville does more than a million dollars' worth of business annually in confections, bakery products and carbonated drinks in a wholesale way. Some of the firms engaged in these lines are among the largest of their kind in the South. Hundreds of tons of candy are annually manufactured in Knoxville and sold all over the South. Reputations of a high order have been built up by candy manufacturers in Knoxville. When these manufacturer's brands appear on packages of candy it means to the public a high-grade product. The manufacturers of the Red Seal Brand Candies have the largest exclusive candy house in the Southern States.

Knoxville supplies a vast amount of the bakery bread used in East Tennessee and even some beyond the borders of East Tennessee, and a vast amount of bottled goods are sold in a wholesale way from this city.

Groceries

The grocery jobbing business of Knoxville amounts to about five millions of dollars annually, and its rapid growth during the last fifteen years, it is believed, will be duplicated in the next ten years by reason of the rapid development of the resources of the patronizing territory of the South. While other cities which do a wholesale grocery business, have territories that have largely reached their natural de-

ELKS HOME, KNOXVILLE

velopment, it can be said of Knoxville's territory that it has scarcely entered upon it. The incoming of new railroads and the consequent development of the coal, timber, iron and other resources, means, of course, more people to be fed from grocery storehouses of Knoxville. As each succeeding year has been better than the former for the grocery business of Knoxville, it is confidently expected that fat years are ahead for a long time to come.

Other Lines

Knoxville does over a million dollar business annually in farm, mill and mine machinery, boilers, engines, threshers, fertilizers and electric supplies and sewing machines.

Wholesale fruit trees and ornamental shrubbery are sold from this city to the extent of about a quarter of a million dollars annually.

About three million dollars' worth of packing house products are shipped to several Southern States.

In wholesale fruits, seeds and produce Knoxville firms do an annual business of half a million dollars.

Knoxville is the largest hardwood mantel market in the United States.

Knoxville is the market for nearly a million tons of coal annually.

A large furniture manufacturing and jobbing center.

The leader in the marble manufacturing industry in the South.

VIEWS ON TENNESSEE AND FRENCH BROAD RIVERS
(Photos by J. E. Thompson)

THE COUNTRY CLUB

FRONT VIEW

SECTION OF THE GRILL ROOM

THE Cherokee Country Club is a social organization, composed of the best people of Knoxville. It owns about thirty-five or forty acres of land on the Kingston Pike, about four miles west of the city.

The Club-house is situated on the left of the pike, and overlooks the beautiful Horse-shoe Bend, of the Tennessee River, the view from the back porch of the Club-house being unsurpassed by any in East Tennessee. On the right of the pike the Club owns about thirty-five acres of land, on which they have a nine-hole golf course and a number of tennis courts.

The Club-house is modern in every respect, having an up-to-date dining-room, kitchen and buffet; also being equipped with bowling alleys, billiard tables, shuffle boards and other amusements. It also has shower baths, lockers for the golf players, and is equipped with its own water and light plant.

The membership of the Club at present is about two hundred and fifty.

The remarkable progress made in developing the Club's property and getting it to its present excellent condition is a tribute to the officers and managers of the Club.

RIVER VIEW FROM REAR PORCH

A CORNER IN THE PARLOR

THE GOLF LINKS

KNOXVILLE HOMES

KNOXVILLE

As an Educational Center

ALTHOUGH many people think of Knoxville as being the center of a district notable for its marble, coal and other mineral deposits, too often they forget that the Queen City of the Mountains has now become an educational center of no small importance. The great influx of strangers from other parts of the country is not due entirely to their belief in the commercial future of this city, but partly, at least, to their feeling that here is an ideal place for them to bring up and educate their children.

At that time this building was the finest structure south of the Ohio River. So elegant was it thought to be that a candidate for office accused his opponent of extravagance for having allowed such high-grade material to be used in the construction of this college edifice.

Through many years of hard struggles the institution gradually rose to the important position which it now occupies in the field of Southern education. It was the first State University in this section to throw open its doors to women.

More than a century ago, in what is now the busiest portion of the city, was established one of the first institutions for higher learning in the South. This was known as Blount College, afterwards East Tennessee University, and now the University of Tennessee. A few years later the institution was moved to its present location, and about 1826 the central building on the campus, now known as Old College, was erected.

Nearly all of the others have since followed in its footsteps. t was the first Southern college to have a Y. M. C. A. building with paid physical instructor and secretary.

Several years ago it established a Summer School for Teachers. This school was reported by *Harper's Weekly* as having a larger attendance than any other school of its kind in the world. At one session more than two thousand students

SCIENCE HALL, UNIVERSITY OF TENNESSEE

were enrolled. The Military Department of the University has always done excellent work. Especially was this shown at the time of the Spanish-American war, when more than fifty commissioned officers of the United States Volunteers were chosen from former Tennessee students. In many other lines graduates of the University are forging their way to the front. It has been but a short time since it happened that the Governor of Tennessee, the Superintendent of Public Instruction, the Adjutant-General, the Commissioner of Agriculture, the Speaker of the Senate, and one of the State Railway Commissioners were all of the alumni of this venerable university.

UNIVERSITY OF TENNESSEE FROM TENNESSEE RIVER

DRIVEWAY AT THE UNIVERSITY OF TENNESSEE

Now, if Knoxville is fortunate in having the cap-stone of the State educational system located in her midst, it is also favored in having such excellent primary and secondary schools. Under the efficient superintendency of the Hon. Seymour Mynderse, formerly State Superintendent of Public Instruction, the city school system will soon be equal to that of any city of like size in the country. At present, somewhat crowded on account of the phenomenal growth of Knoxville, the schools cannot do quite so well as will be possible when the new buildings under course of construction are completed. The city is to be congratulated on its good fortune in securing so capable a man to place at the head of its schools. The most modern methods of teaching have been introduced wherever practicable. In this place it might be well to mention the excellent County High School, recently established in a well known suburb. Knox County deserves much credit for the

TENNESSEE RIVER NEAR UNIVERSITY OF TENNESSEE

progressive spirit which prompted its County Court to provide for such a high school.

In the western part of the city is located the well known boarding and day school for boys, called Baker-Himel, from the names of its founders. This school takes only one hundred and twenty-five pupils. So excellent has been its work that at no time has one of its graduates failed to pass an entrance examination into Yale, Princeton, Annapolis, or any other of flourishing private schools are maintained. Numerous kindergartens provide for the smallest children.

The Knoxville Business College, McAllen's, and Draughon's, provide amply for the commercial education of those who are looking forward to an active business life, while those who are anxious to cultivate the social and musical bent will find here a number of schools devoted to dancing and music.

BAKER-HIMEL, A BOARDING SCHOOL FOR BOYS

CENTRAL Y. M. C. A. BUILDING

the great American institutions of learning. One of its graduates was the second Cecil Rhodes student to be appointed from the State. This school takes pupils of all ages. Similar in character to Baker-Himel School is the East Tennessee Female Institute for young ladies. This school also has won an excellent record. Several other private schools are located in the city, most of them for small children. Under the auspices of the Catholic and the German Lutheran churches

The Knoxville Medical College bears an excellent reputation and affords a local opening for the student with professional inclinations. It has a competent corps of instructors, composed of leading physicians, surgeons, and specialists of this community. No educational summary of Knoxville, however brief, would be complete were we to fail to mention the Knoxville College, an institution of good standing founded for the colored race.

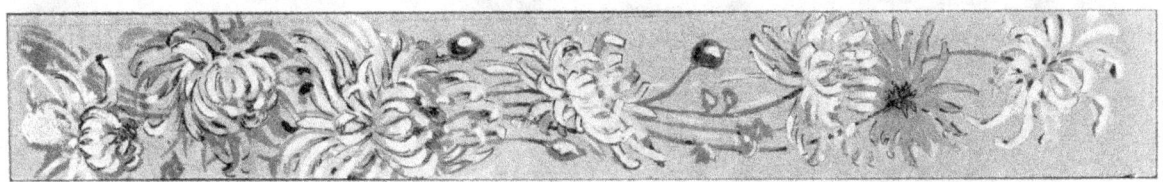

KNOXVILLE PUBLIC SCHOOL BUILDINGS

KNOXVILLE'S BANKS

KNOXVILLE has nine banks, with over $12,000,000 on deposit. In 1906 the clearings amounted to $74,356,153.65, and will reach $80,000,000 for the present fiscal year.

Two new bank buildings are now under construction. The Mechanics Bank & Trust Company, recently organized, is erecting a handsome five-story building, and work has commenced on the ten-story steel frame building of the Knoxville Banking & Trust Company.

Knoxville has four National Banks—The East Tennessee National, City National, Third National and Holston National banks. Besides these are the Union Bank, Knox County Bank and Trust Co., Merchants Bank, and the two previously mentioned.

No city of its size in the South has as much money in its banks, such large clearings, or stronger and more reliable banks than has Knoxville.

Knoxville is the banking headquarters of the rich Southern Appalachian territory; that is, for Southeastern Kentucky, and Southwestern Virginia, Western North Carolina, Northern Georgia and East Tennessee. This is the field where the greatest fortunes of the South are to be made in the future and where wealth will accumulate faster.

The growth of the financial strength of the banks of Knoxville can be clearly seen from an examination of the sworn reports, which are issued from time to time, of both the National and the State banks.

Every bank has shown steady and strong growth. Some of the older ones have reached mammoth proportions. All are directed by conservative, able men, who have the utmost confidence of the people. Though conservative and cautious in management, the banks are progressive. A healthy rivalry exists. Eyes are open to every opportunity, and wherever a safe proposition comes to the front one or more of the progressive bankers are there ready to meet it. All of the liberality consistent with good business methods is shown.

It speaks well for Knoxville that those banks which have saving accounts are showing great advancement. The laboring men, those who are on salaries and all who can save are taking advantage of the opportunities afforded for laying by something for the future. The banks go hard after this business. Some of them issue monthly pamphlets full of the most interesting matter and well suited to arouse the thriftless to the duty of saving. Many people in Knoxville will be grateful in after years that they were induced to open a savings account.

Increase in Bank Clearings

The following table shows the great increases made in Knoxville's bank clearings from 1896 to 1906. The gain for the ten years was about 350 per cent:

1906	$74,353,153.65
1905	63,576,086.17
1904	61,440,172.55
1903	58,350,311.98
1902	40,730,026.31
1901	32,496,361.73
1900	28,834,248.48
1899	29,411,520.65
1898	26,812,252.03
1897	22,734,344.05
1896	21,457,089.47

The bank deposits of Knoxville have doubled in ten years.

DRESS PARADE, UNIVERSITY OF TENNESSEE

THE KNOXVILLE BOARD OF TRADE

CARY F. SPENCE
President of the Board of Trade

KNOXVILLE has a Board of Trade composed of workers. There are several hundred members of this organization who realize that the good of each is inextricably bound up in the good of all, and they make it a part of their business to pull for Knoxville.

Knoxville's growth is steady, healthy and permanent. She has now a population of about 85,000, and a glance at the hundreds of new buildings throughout the city, and especially in the near suburbs, clearly indicates a city within five years of 100,000 people. Every member of the Board of Trade is working to this end.

A city of 100,000 means not only an increase in the number of people; it means more factories, more business houses and residences; more and better streets and highways; improvements in the city and an increase in the value of present buildings. It means improved facilities, better transportation, more railroads, the opening and developing of more mines and quarries and the growth of our present industries.

Knoxville's advantages and resources are the envy of many sections of this country not so fortunately situated. She has at her doors an abundance of coal, iron, marble and timber, and it is the province of this Board of Trade to present these facts to the outside world in such a manner that we may induce additional capital to locate here. Her climate, the year round, is not surpassed by any country on the globe, and her advantages are many.

Baumann Bros., Architects.

H. W. HALL
Vice President of the Board of Trade

D. C. CHAPMAN
Second Vice President of the Board of Trade

Some Things the Board of Trade is Trying to Do

Induce more manufacturers to locate here; push Knoxville-made goods; co-operate in business and municipal affairs; advertise Knoxville as she is to the world; create more civic pride; secure more water and better fire protection; promote the good feeling existing here between capital and labor; assist the city's officers in enforcing the laws; increase our library facilities; extend the privileges of the city; build an auditorium; encourage and assist desirable immigration to East Tennessee, and to help everything that helps Knoxville.

The Board of Trade has an efficient Secretary, and a number of committees that discharge their duties in a way that brings the most gratifying results. The organization has been fortunate in its selection of officers and boards of directors. Col. Spence, who now holds the office of President, is the right man in the right place. He is for Knoxville, first, last and all of the time, and avails himself of every opportunity to promote the interests of the city and to keep up enthusiasm on the part of members.

A vast amount of advertising literature is sent out by the Board of Trade, and the Secretary is kept busy replying to letters from parties in all parts of the country who are looking for good locations in the South for homes and various industries.

Movements relating to railroads, the improvement of waterways, the conservation of forests—everything pertaining to the general welfare—are brought up for discussion at the meetings of this organization, and where action is deemed advisable, it is taken in the way that seems most certain to produce the desired results, regardless of the expense and labor involved.

The officers of the Board of Trade are, Cary F. Spence, president; H. W. Hall, vice-president; D. C. Chapman, second vice-president; and James A. Hensley, secretary.

MANUFACTURERS' AND PRODUCERS' ASSOCIATION

THE objects and principles of this Association, as set forth in its Constitution, are as follows, viz.:

"To secure to the manufacturing and producing industries of Knoxville and adjacent territory the safest protection, the most conducive legislation and the most thorough development of our manufacturing and producing interests, and also to develop by promoting better acquaintance among members, a social and mutual interest, which will advance, extend and protect the business of our manufacturers and producers."

The fundamental principles are fair dealing as the basic principle on which the Association rests in all its relations, with the purpose and desire to encourage and protect every interest of manufacturing and productive industries, and of all in any way engaged therein, and it is not its object or intent to regulate or control personal liberties, and the Association pledges itself to oppose all legislation not in accord with these principles.

The Association was chartered under the laws of Tennessee June 23, 1903, with James Maynard, Oscar M. Tate, D. M. Rose, Thomas R. Price, J. Allen Smith, R. P. Gettys, Hugh W. Sanford, Arthur Groves, and Russell A. Clapp as charter members, and organized with a membership of some fifty.

Mr. James Maynard was elected President. The rule having been adopted of no president succeeding himself, at the June, 1904, meeting, Mr. Oscar M. Tate was elected President. He was succeeded in 1905 by Mr. J. E. Willard, and he in 1906 by Wm. P. Chamberlain. The present incumbent of the office having been elected in June, 1907, is Mr. W. J. Savage.

Early in the history of the Association a Freight Claim Bureau was established under the direction of the Secretary, and this has proven to be a very valuable feature. In order that its benefits might be extended to others than manufacturers, an associate membership was provided for, early in 1907, and this has been taken advantage of by many of the larger shippers in mercantile lines, and is being appreciated.

The Association in all directions indicated in the objects for which it was organized, and has since been conducted, has been very helpful to the members, as well as to non-affiliated manufacturers, inimical legislation has been lessened, informa-

W. J. SAVAGE
President of the Manufacturers' and Producers' Association

JAMES MAYNARD
First President of the Manufacturers' and Producers' Association

OSCAR M. TATE
President of Manufacturers' and Producers' Association in 1905

tion as to the advantages Knoxville possesses as a manufacturing center has been furnished, and backed by personal efforts, and mutual and social interests have been strengthened.

Under the present efficient oversight and direction of President W. J. Savage, and the active and intelligent work of the Secretary, J. M. Starrett, the organization is now in a most flourishing condition and its membership steadily increasing. The Association occupies very desirable quarters on the office floor of the Imperial Hotel, where the Secretary can be found, or addressed, if information along lines of work of the Association is desired.

WILLIAM P. CHAMBERLAIN
President of the Manufacturers' and Producers' Association in 1906

THE COMMERCIAL CLUB OF KNOXVILLE

THE Commercial Club, formed January 21, 1895, "For the Advancement of the Jobbing Interests of Knoxville," is the oldest business organization in the city. J. T. McTeer was the first president, and the Constitution and By-Laws were drafted by R. S. Hazen and H. Coffin.

The following firms attached their signatures to an agreement to abide by the Constitution, By-Laws, Rules and Regulations, as adopted by the required majority:

Cowan, McClung & Co.   S. B. Newman & Co.
Chapman, White, Lyons Co.   Cullen & Newman.

KNOXVILLE CHURCHES (Photos by J. E. Thompson)

Haynes Bros.
Hazen & Lotspeich.
Greer Machinery Co.
C. M. McClung & Co.
Littlefield, Steere & Sanders.
W. B. Lockett & Co.
Allen, Stephenson & Co.
Spence & Co.
Ogden Bros. & Co.
Knoxville Knitting Mills Co.
Shields Bros.
Davis, Brownlee & Chumbley.
Powers, Little & Co.
Knaffl & Locke.
Haynes, Henson & Co.
J. S. Shields & Co.
McMillan, Hazen & Co.
Daniel Briscoe, Bro. & Co.
M. L. Ross & Co.
Dick, McMillan & Co.
McTeers, Hood & Co.
Sterchi Bros.
W. W. Woodruff & Co.
Roney, Arnold & Co.
Knoxville Provision & Sugar Co.
Graves & King.
Sanford, Chamberlain & Albers.
Hill, Lloyd & Co.
Perry & Co.
Howard Karnes.
Cowan, Magill & Co.
Knoxville Trunk & Harness Co.
Kaiser Bros.
J. Allen Smith & Co.
Scott Bros.
George Brown.
George & Murphy.

The following were the members of the first Executive Committee of the Club: J. Pike Powers, P. J. Briscoe, C. M McClung, M. S. McClellan, A. J. Albers, J. P. Haynes, R. S Hazen and C. Cullen.

J. E. Hickman was the first Secretary and Treasurer of the organization, serving until the fall of 1895, when he was succeeded by W. H. Kephart. At that time, and until June, 1897, the meetings of the Club were held in the rooms of the Chamber of Commerce, one secretary acting for both organizations. Mr. Kephart was succeeded as Secretary of the Commercial Club and Chamber of Commerce by H. M. Branson. On June 12, 1897, Mr. J. S. Shields brought before the Club a proposition to separate this organization from the Chamber of Commerce and elect W. M. Goodman, Editor of The Business Magazine, Secretary and Treasurer of the Club. The proposition was accepted, and soon afterwards a room was secured in the Lawson-McGhee Library building and the Club moved to new quarters.

The officers of the Club are elected each year. The names of those who have held the office of President follow:

(A. J. Albers, chairman of first meeting called to consider proposition to organize Club).

Presidents

J. T. McTeer, January, 1895, to February, 1897.
J. S. Shields, February, 1897, to December, 1897.
M. D. Arnold, December, 1897, to December, 1898.
P. J. Briscoe, Sr., December, 1898, to December, 1899.
J. Pike Powers, December, 1899, to December, 1901.
A. J. Albers, December, 1901, to December, 1903.
J. Pike Powers, December, 1903, to December, 1905.
Geo. W. Murphy, December, 1905, to December, 1907.

Vice-Presidents

J. S. Shields,
M. D. Arnold,   Jan., 1895, to Feb., 1897.

P. J. Briscoe, Sr.,
E. E. McMillan,   Feb., 1897, to Dec., 1897.

A. J. Albers,
R. M. Rhea,   Dec., 1897, to Dec., 1898.

R. S. Hazen,
J. Allen Smith,   Dec., 1898, to Dec., 1899.

R. M. Rhea,
A. J. Albers,   Dec., 1899, to Dec., 1901.

M. D. Arnold,
G. J. Ashe,   Dec., 1901, to Dec., 1902.

R. M. Rhea,
J. E. Briscoe,   Dec., 1902, to Dec., 1903.

GEORGE W. MURPHY
President of the Commercial Club

M. S. McClellan,
David Chapman,   Dec., 1903, to Dec., 1905.

Edward Henegar,
C. J. McClung,   Dec., 1905, to Dec., 1906.

Edward Henegar,
Jesse Thomas,   Dec., 1906, to Dec., 1907.

The Commercial Club was chartered under the laws of Tennessee on September 9, 1897, by J. S. Shields, Edward Henegar, W. B. Lockett, W. E. Gibbins and W. M. Goodman. Organized for the advancement of the jobbing interests of Knoxville, it has succeeded well in all of its undertakings. The business coming to Knoxville jobbers through the Club has shown a large increase each year. In many instances its field has been broadened so as to include, with the interests of jobbers, the interests of all business people of the city. The minutes of the Club show, mainly, numerous plans suggested and put in operation to induce merchants to visit this market, but they show other things worthy of notice. For instance, in 1897 we find the Club in litigation with the railroads on account of discrimination in freight rates against this market. The Railroad Commission of the State of Tennessee gave judgment in favor of the Club on every point contested and a more satisfactory adjustment of rates was the final outcome of the work of the organization. In December, 1897, an appropriation was made by the Club to secure steamboat service between Knoxville and St. Louis, with freight rates not to exceed two-thirds of the railroad rates between the two cities. The members of the Club subscribed to a fund for this purpose, but the steamboat people were unable to carry out the plan proposed. In March, 1898, a movement was inaugurated by the Club to secure interchangeable mileage over Southern roads. On July 18, 1898, a meeting of the Club was called to confer with Lieutenant Horace Van Deventer in regard to the purchase of army supplies in Knoxville instead of Chicago, as had been proposed. It was shown that Chicago prices were exhorbitant. A committee was appointed to protest against the purchase of supplies in Chicago for a regiment stationed at Knoxville, and a citizens' meeting was called to take further action. Good business for this city was the result. On May 8th, 1900, the Club held a special meeting to arrange a parade in honor of Admiral George Dewey, who visited the city the following week. October 19, 1900, a meeting was held to discuss new telephone rates. A committee was appointed to learn the wishes of business men in regard to taking out one of the phones in use in the city. On January 22, 1901, the Club adopted resolutions endorsing the annual appropriation for fast mail service between New York and New Orleans, via Atlanta, and urging the Tennessee delegation in Congress to use their influence for the continuance of the appropriation. Resolutions were unanimously adopted at this meeting concerning a forest reserve to be established in the Southern Appalachian region, and copies of resolutions were mailed to members of Congress. At a meeting held March 21, 1901, action was taken looking to the passage of a bill before the Legislature of Tennessee providing terms upon which sales of goods in bulk might be made. On September 14, 1901, a special meeting of the Club was called to take suitable action on the death of President McKinley, at which some strong resolutions were passed condemning anarchists.

In February, 1904, the Club took up the question of increased insurance rates on business property, promises from companies to reduce these rates following efforts of the Club which resulted in better fire protection. On May 30, 1905, there was another meeting of the Club to consider the removal of the "Pink Slip" from insurance policies, and demands for its removal were renewed. On May 31, 1906, the question of fire insurance and fire-fighting facilities was again brought up, and a committee was appointed to look into the matter. The members of this committee, Messrs. W. T. Claiborne, S. D. Coykendall, Geo. McTeer, Edward Henegar and H. M. Johnston, carried on their investigations in a most thorough and satisfactory manner, and they were continued on this committee and asked to place the results of their investigations before the other business organizations of the city and secure their cooperation.

Few claims have been made by the Club and its committees, and little publicity has been given to their work, but they deserve great credit for what they have undertaken and for what they have accomplished for the public good.

The officers of the Commercial Club, elected at the last annual meeting, are: President, George W. Murphy; Vice-President, Edward Henegar; Second Vice-President, Jesse Thomas; Secretary and Treasurer, W. M. Goodman.

Members of the Commercial Club

Wholesale Dry Goods.—Daniel Briscoe, Bro. & Co., Brown, Payne, Deaver & Co., Cowan, McClung & Co., Hicks-Hodge-Jamerson Co.

Wholesale Boots and Shoes.—Arnold, Henegar, Doyle & Co., Haynes-Henson Shoe Co., McMillan, Hazen & Co.

Wholesale Clothing.—Bickley, McClure & Co., Claiborne, Tate & Cowan, Gillespie, Shields & Co., J. T. McTeer Clothing Co., Powers, Little & Co., Suttle & Beeler.

Wholesale Hats and Caps.—W. A. Clark & Co., S. C. Dismukes & Co., McCulley Hat Co.

Wholesale Grocers.—Chastain, Davis & Co., Borches & Co., The H. T. Hackney Co., Hazen & Lotspeich Co., Kaiser Bros. (also fruits and vegetables.)

Wholesale Hardware.—House-Hasson Hardware Co., C. M. McClung & Co., W. W. Woodruff Hardware Co.

Wholesale Drugs.—Chapman, White, Lyons Co., Sanford, Chamberlain & Albers Co.

Wholesale Notions.—Daniel Briscoe, Bro. & Co., Brown, Payne, Deaver & Co., Cowan, McClung & Co., Hicks-Hodge-Jamerson Co.

Agricultural Implements, Seeds, Etc.—Broyles, McClellan & Lackey Co., C. M. McClung & Co., W. W. Woodruff Hardware Co.

Printers and Bookbinders.—Bean, Warters & Co., Gaut-Ogden Co., Knoxville Printing & Box Co., S. B. Newman & Co.

Wholesale Queensware.—Chas. C. Cullen & Co., Hill, Lloyd & Co., Sterchi Bros.

Stoves and Tinware.—Hill, Lloyd & Co., House-Hasson Hardware Co., C. M. McClung & Co., W. W. Woodruff Hardware Co.

Hosiery.—Knox Knitting Mills Co.

Machinery and Electric Supplies.—John G. Duncan Co., C. M. McClung & Co., W. W. Woodruff Hardware Co.

Manufacturing Confectioners.—Littlefield & Steere Co., Peter Kern Co.

Wholesale Furniture.—Allen, Stephenson & Co., W. N. Smith, Sterchi Bros., Vance Furniture Co.

Furniture Manufacturers.—The Proctor Furniture Co.

Harness and Saddlery.—Broyles, McClellan & Lackey Co., Howard Karnes, C. M. McClung & Co.

Clothing Manufacturers.—Claiborne, Tate & Cowan. Suttle & Beeler.

Flour, Meal, Etc.—Knoxville City Mills, Scott Mill Co.

Mantels, Grates, Tiles, Etc.—King Mantel Co.

Trunks, Traveling Bags, Etc.—The Whittle Trunk and Bag Co.

Cement, Sewer Pipe, Tile, Etc.—Chandler & Co.

Manufacturers Pants, Overalls.—National Manufacturing Co., Regal Manufacturing Co., Standard Clothing Co., Smith, Neal & Co., Suttle & Beeler, Union Manufacturing Co. Briscoe Manufacturing Co.

Bread, Cakes, Etc.—Peter Kern Co.

Skirt Manufacturers.—McBee-Hambright Mfg. Co.

REAL ESTATE

THE development of the real estate business in Knoxville has been along legitimate and safe lines. There has been nothing like a boom for many years. The growth of the city during the past decade was healthy and substantial, and the rapid progress that is being made at this time is the result of general business activity and the good opportunities for profitable investment that are offered here.

Buying real estate in and around Knoxville is a safe business, and one from which excellent returns are assured. City property is bringing very high prices compared with the prices ruling four or five years ago, but there will be great increases in value in four or five years from now. In the suburbs, however, is where the investor can pick up desirable property at low prices. The demand a few years hence will be for suburban residence and factory sites, and those who purchase property of this kind now will be able to dispose of it at a considerable advance.

A great deal of money has been made in suburban real estate. Lonsdale, Lincoln Park, Oakwood and other thickly settled suburbs were old fields and woods lots a few years ago. The lands were purchased at so much per acre, laid off in lots, with streets and sidewalks, and sold at prices that yielded large profits to the promoters. A number of excellent locations for suburban additions can be found on and near car lines, and the land can be bought at prices ranging from two hundred to five hundred dollars per acre. Some of this property lies in the best suburban residence sections, fronting on good macadamized roads, with river view.

Among the best real estate propositions here are timber, mineral and farm lands. Farming pays as well in East Tennessee as in any section of the South, but, as is the case in all parts of the country, many young men and boys are drawn to the city, with the result that excellent farms are thrown on the market at prices far below their value.

To all who are looking Southward we will say, you can buy a home in Knoxville today for less money than the same property will sell for a year hence. You can purchase business property, farm, timber or mineral lands as an investment with the certainty of profiting by increasing demand and value.

Here are some facts of interest to home-seekers:

Knoxville has an excellent medium of climate, splendid drainage, both natural and artificial; it is situated high and dry on its hills; it has its paved streets, flushed clean; it requires sewer connection from property owners; it has an excellent board of health; a number of noted physicians; two splendidly equipped hospitals; it is well shaded with yard trees that give a park-like appearance to the whole city. Its death rate last year was 14.55, a rate that is made larger than normal because the hospitals are widely used by patients coming from a distance of several hundred miles, and the deaths are credited to Knoxville in the reports, because the negro quarters carry a death rate almost double that of the white, and because Knoxville is the mecca of old people of surrounding territory.

Knoxville is situated 1,000 feet above sea level, in the heart of the Valley of East Tennessee, sheltered from destructive storms by the mountains; is the second coolest city in the South during the summer months and cooler than the larger cities of the North. Average annual temperature, 57 degrees; summer, 74; winter, 40; spring, 57; autumn, 58. Average annual rainfall, 52 inches.

Knoxville is known as a city of churches. Perhaps more people attend church in Knoxville than any city of its size in the country. The generous support which is given the church by the members and the public at large, makes it possible to obtain the best preachers.

Knoxville Central Y. M. C. A. owns a splendid building and equipment worth as much as $75,000; has a thousand members and is a factor of great moral influence among young men. In Knoxville there is a strong Railroad Y. M. C. A., supported by railroad men who make their homes here at the headquarters of the Knoxville division of the Southern and of the L. & N. railroads.

The Young Women's Christian Association maintains a home for working girls and the Woman's Christian Association has charge of the general charities of the city.

Knoxville has ten educational institutions aside from its excellent public schools, viz.; the University of Tennessee, one of the foremost universities in the South in both technical and classical education; the Summer School of the South, which meets annually during the summer at the University of Tennessee, the greatest school for teachers in the South, and having an average enrollment of over two thousand; the Baker-Himel preparatory school for boys, having a limited scholarship of about one hundred and doing a specially high grade work; the East Tennessee Female Institute, a fashionable and high grade school for girls; the Tennessee Deaf and Dumb School, a State institution educating the deaf and dumb of both colors of the State, and having a splendid equipment; the Lincoln Memorial Medical College (formerly the Tennessee Medical College), an institution turning out each year a number of well equipped physicians; the Knoxville College, one of the largest colored institutions of the South, and doing a high class of work; the Knoxville Business College, one of the oldest and largest business colleges of the South; McAllen's Business College, a well established, high grade commercial college; the Draughon's Business College, branch of a well known system of colleges, and the Knox County High School, located at Fountain City, a suburb of Knoxville.

Knoxville's Million Dollar Shoe House

Haynes-Henson Shoe Company

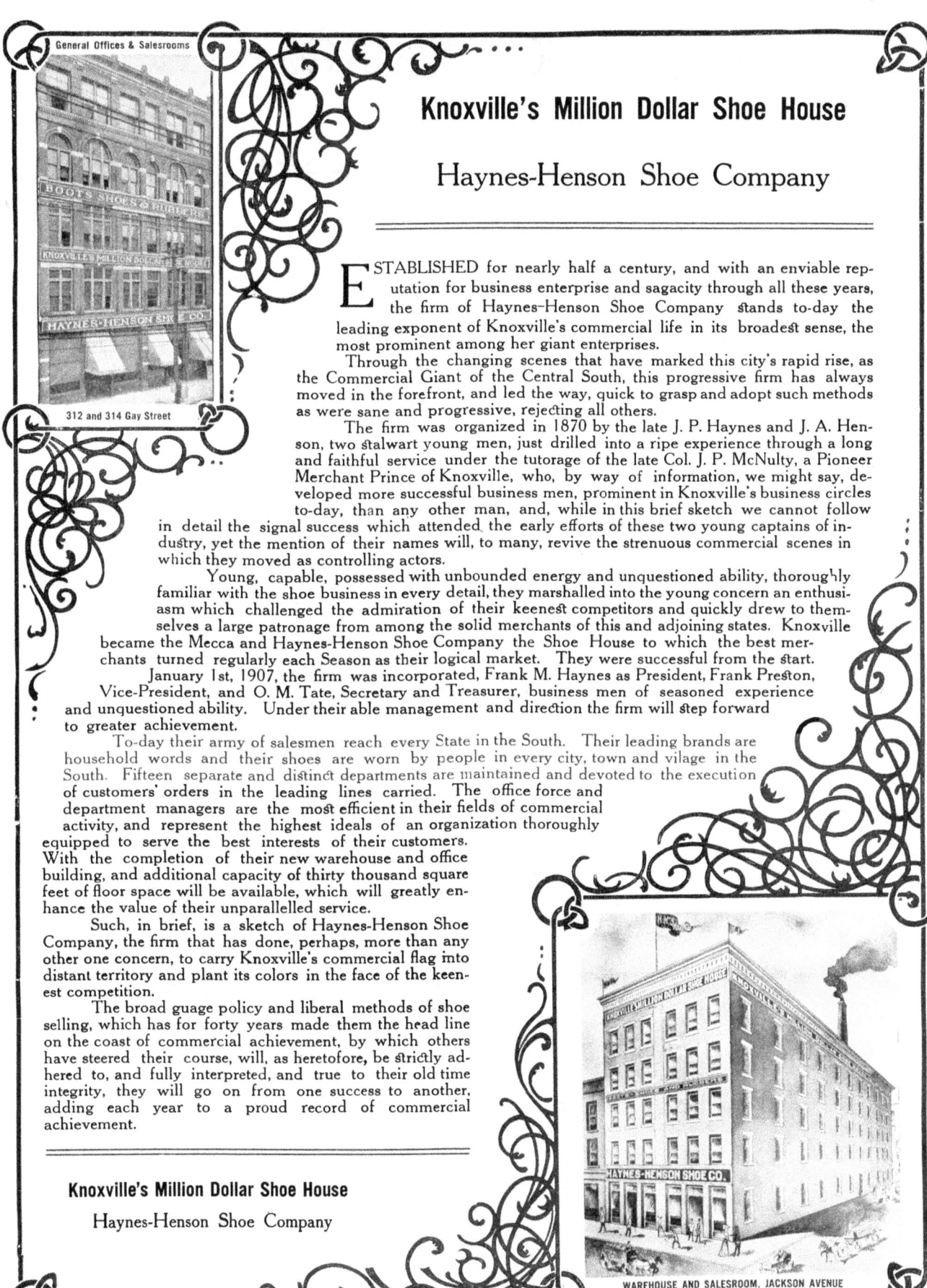

General Offices & Salesrooms
312 and 314 Gay Street

ESTABLISHED for nearly half a century, and with an enviable reputation for business enterprise and sagacity through all these years, the firm of Haynes-Henson Shoe Company stands to-day the leading exponent of Knoxville's commercial life in its broadest sense, the most prominent among her giant enterprises.

Through the changing scenes that have marked this city's rapid rise, as the Commercial Giant of the Central South, this progressive firm has always moved in the forefront, and led the way, quick to grasp and adopt such methods as were sane and progressive, rejecting all others.

The firm was organized in 1870 by the late J. P. Haynes and J. A. Henson, two stalwart young men, just drilled into a ripe experience through a long and faithful service under the tutorage of the late Col. J. P. McNulty, a Pioneer Merchant Prince of Knoxville, who, by way of information, we might say, developed more successful business men, prominent in Knoxville's business circles to-day, than any other man, and, while in this brief sketch we cannot follow in detail the signal success which attended the early efforts of these two young captains of industry, yet the mention of their names will, to many, revive the strenuous commercial scenes in which they moved as controlling actors.

Young, capable, possessed with unbounded energy and unquestioned ability, thoroughly familiar with the shoe business in every detail, they marshalled into the young concern an enthusiasm which challenged the admiration of their keenest competitors and quickly drew to themselves a large patronage from among the solid merchants of this and adjoining states. Knoxville became the Mecca and Haynes-Henson Shoe Company the Shoe House to which the best merchants turned regularly each Season as their logical market. They were successful from the start.

January 1st, 1907, the firm was incorporated, Frank M. Haynes as President, Frank Preston, Vice-President, and O. M. Tate, Secretary and Treasurer, business men of seasoned experience and unquestioned ability. Under their able management and direction the firm will step forward to greater achievement.

To-day their army of salesmen reach every State in the South. Their leading brands are household words and their shoes are worn by people in every city, town and vilage in the South. Fifteen separate and distinct departments are maintained and devoted to the execution of customers' orders in the leading lines carried. The office force and department managers are the most efficient in their fields of commercial activity, and represent the highest ideals of an organization thoroughly equipped to serve the best interests of their customers. With the completion of their new warehouse and office building, and additional capacity of thirty thousand square feet of floor space will be available, which will greatly enhance the value of their unparallelled service.

Such, in brief, is a sketch of Haynes-Henson Shoe Company, the firm that has done, perhaps, more than any other one concern, to carry Knoxville's commercial flag into distant territory and plant its colors in the face of the keenest competition.

The broad guage policy and liberal methods of shoe selling, which has for forty years made them the head line on the coast of commercial achievement, by which others have steered their course, will, as heretofore, be strictly adhered to, and fully interpreted, and true to their old time integrity, they will go on from one success to another, adding each year to a proud record of commercial achievement.

Knoxville's Million Dollar Shoe House
Haynes-Henson Shoe Company

WAREHOUSE AND SALESROOM, JACKSON AVENUE

KNOXVILLE'S TWO MILLION DOLLAR DRY GOODS AND NOTION HOUSE

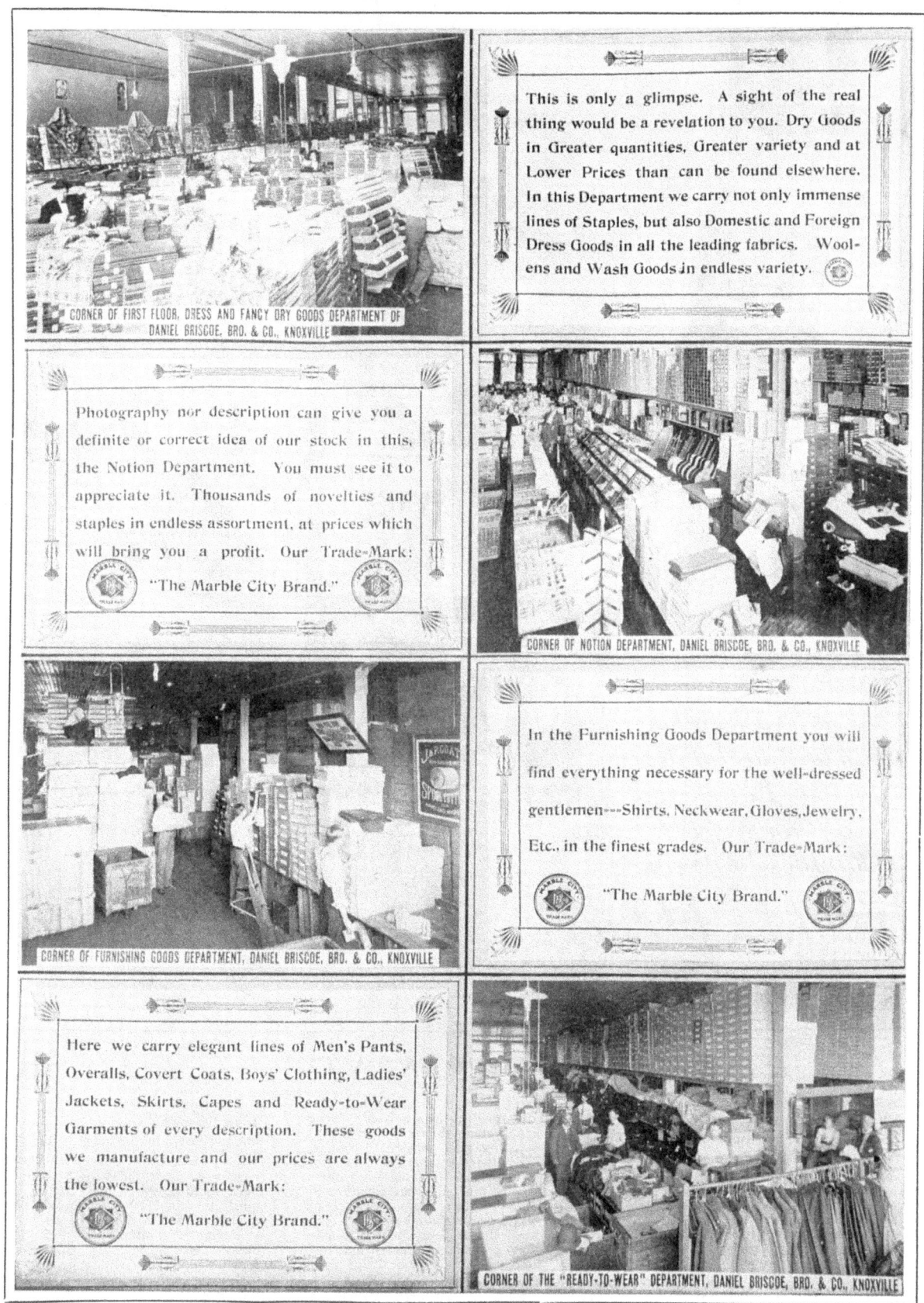

This is only a glimpse. A sight of the real thing would be a revelation to you. Dry Goods in Greater quantities, Greater variety and at Lower Prices than can be found elsewhere. In this Department we carry not only immense lines of Staples, but also Domestic and Foreign Dress Goods in all the leading fabrics. Woolens and Wash Goods in endless variety.

CORNER OF FIRST FLOOR, DRESS AND FANCY DRY GOODS DEPARTMENT OF DANIEL BRISCOE, BRO. & CO., KNOXVILLE

Photography nor description can give you a definite or correct idea of our stock in this, the Notion Department. You must see it to appreciate it. Thousands of novelties and staples in endless assortment, at prices which will bring you a profit. Our Trade=Mark: "The Marble City Brand."

CORNER OF NOTION DEPARTMENT, DANIEL BRISCOE, BRO. & CO., KNOXVILLE

In the Furnishing Goods Department you will find everything necessary for the well=dressed gentlemen---Shirts, Neckwear, Gloves, Jewelry, Etc., in the finest grades. Our Trade=Mark: "The Marble City Brand."

CORNER OF FURNISHING GOODS DEPARTMENT, DANIEL BRISCOE, BRO. & CO., KNOXVILLE

Here we carry elegant lines of Men's Pants, Overalls, Covert Coats, Boys' Clothing, Ladies' Jackets, Skirts, Capes and Ready-to-Wear Garments of every description. These goods we manufacture and our prices are always the lowest. Our Trade=Mark: "The Marble City Brand."

CORNER OF THE "READY-TO-WEAR" DEPARTMENT, DANIEL BRISCOE, BRO. & CO., KNOXVILLE

Supplying You With Merchandise That Pays More Than The Usual Profit

DOLLARS FOR DEALERS

A BEAUTY WITH 18-KARAT VALUE

DOLLARS FOR DEALERS

A SMART MODEL FOR SOUTHERN GENTLEMEN

"American Queen," over 30 styles, Fashioned With a Careful Regard for the Latest and Most Advanced Ideas in Feminine Footwear.

"The Arnold," over 60 styles, comprising Many New and Exclusive Designs, that will do Credit to the Best Store in the Land.

Arnold, Henegar, Doyle & Company
KNOXVILLE'S YOUNGEST AND LEADING SHOE HOUSE

THE PAST

The makers of this Souvenir Book proudly point to the artistic pages before you, and desire to print a word regarding the past present and future policy of the progressive firm of Arnold, Henegar, Doyle & Co. "Vim, Values and Volume," their first slogan, has been made good, thus setting the pace for others. Vim, which entered into every department of their business from the beginning, together with high shoe values as their standard, naturally brought their great increase in volume. They stepped to the front the first season, and have ever since doggedly maintained their position.

THE PRESENT

The present position of this young firm in the shoe world is firmly fixed. They have accomplished in thirteen years a reputation, standing and business volume, greater than many Southern houses two and three times their years. With their determined way that wins, an ambition to have better and better shoes each season for their customers, and the good luck Horse-Shoe Brand trade-mark that "spells success," they go steadily onward and upward. These and other good things connected with HORSE-SHOE Brand Shoes, and their advertising methods, account for their continual gains.

THE FUTURE

The survival of the fittest brings to the front those able to give mind and body to one purpose, and pursue it to the final end. It is said of this firm that their purpose is to make their shoes the best known and most satisfactory on the market, and are quick to adopt every improved idea and method. With a financial standing second to none; with able men at the head of every department, and the unshakable foundation already laid, it is easy to forecast their business future, and we predict for them still greater achievements in coming years.
—THE EDITORS

A Business-Building, Money-Making Educational Proposition

Every merchant would like to know more about how to buy goods; how to display goods to the best advantage; how to sell goods at a profit; how to advertise; how to win customers, and how to keep them. Learning by experience is slow work. Why not take advantage of the experience of others? The world's best buyers, best window trimmers, best advertisers, and best salesmen tell the merchant readers of The Business Magazine what they know about business-building as carried on through their special departments.

It costs us thousands of dollars each year to get this information. The merchant pays $2.00 a year for the magazine —a little more than the cost of the white paper—with this valuable fund of knowledge and experience thrown in.

The merchant who reads The Business Magazine carefully finds the $2.00 spent for a year's subscription the best investment he can make. Winning one new customer—making one good sale—as a result of ideas advanced by the leading retailers of the country—he has his money back, together with knowledge that will be of benefit to him as long as he is in business.

It is not a question of expense—this subscription proposition—it is one of investment, and an investment that no merchant can afford not to make.

The Business Magazine points the way to success—shows the reader how to improve his business right along day after day—how to utilize things that are allowed to go to waste and turn loss into profit.

Furthermore, it covers the whole field of business, and gives reliable information concerning all lines of commercial and industrial work in all parts of the world.

Every copy worth more than the subscription price of twelve numbers. See what others say.

PERRY
8 Spruce St., New York.

In a single case, an article you published contained information which brought me in cash more than enough to pay the subscription price for ten years. But I made use of that information. Yours truly,

Edward W. Perry

SMOOT BROS. & ROGERS,
Salisbury, N. C.

The Business Magazine, Knoxville, Tenn.

Gentlemen:—We take genuine pleasure in saying that your Magazine is, in our opinion, the most entertaining business Magazine on the American Continent. We have taken, paid for and read it for years and always with keen interest. There is not a dull line in it. It is brimful of wholesome and profitable reading for men in every line of business.

Yours very truly, *Smoot Bros. Rogers*

SEND $2.00 AND LET YOUR SUBSCRIPTION BEGIN NOW

The Business Magazine Pub. Co., Incorporated,   Knoxville, Tenn.

505-507 W. Jackson Avenue
Erected 1893

C. M. McCLUNG & CO.
INCORPORATED

HARDWARE, MILL AND MINE SUPPLIES, STOVES, TINWARE, VEHICLES, SPORTING GOODS.

Knoxville - - Tennessee

EXCLUSIVELY WHOLESALE

501-503 W. Jackson Avenue
1903 Addition

View of Offices, Showing General Correspondence Department

509 W. Jackson Avenue
1896 Addition

C. M. McCLUNG & CO., through an Excellent Organization, Efficient Service, Comprehensive Stocks, and Courteous Treatment, have become not only the largest Hardware Jobbers, but also the largest Jobbers in any line in East Tennessee, which is an unusual achievement for Hardware Distributors in any Section. Their Competent Force of Traveling Salesmen cover completely East Tennessee, Southeastern Kentucky, Southwest Virginia, Western North Carolina, North Georgia and Alabama.

Through their MAIL ORDER DEPARTMENT, which is thoroughly organized, they receive an immense volume of business by carrying an Enormous Stock, embracing many lines of Merchandise. On every sale they guarantee the best of Goods at lowest Prices.

Stove Foundry on Knoxville & Ohio
Railroad Tracks

Cowan, McClung & Company

Importers and Jobbers of Dry Goods and Notions

THE pioneer house of its kind and today the unquestioned leader in its line, is the proud position held by Cowan, McClung & Company, importers and jobbers of dry goods, notions, ladies' and men's furnishings. Established in 1830, this firm has grown to such magnitude that its different departments occupy nearly two acres of floor space, more actual area than is used by any other firm in the same line in Knoxville. It is not too much to say that Cowan, McClung & Company are more familiar with the trade needs and trade conditions of this territory than any business concern in the South. For years, for decades, for almost a century, their traveling men, and members of the firm as well, have gone into every nook and corner of the jobbing territory of Knoxville and have become intimately acquainted with the peculiar wants of each locality and of each merchant. It is by this knowledge that they are able to co-operate with their customers, and it is an undoubted fact that, because of this, their customers are by far the most successful in the South. The old proverb of goods well bought being half sold is truly shown in the success of merchants who do all their buying from Cowan, McClung & Co.

Another powerful factor in the growth of this mammoth concern was the determination, made years ago, that each year's business must show an increase over that of the preceding year. The result is that it is today doing the greatest business in its history. Its aggressive policies have kept it years in advance of its time; but, while the most up-to-date and progressive methods are pursued, it has never abandoned its original aim of honorable dealing with each and every customer, large or small, in each and every transaction, large or small. It might be truly said that this is the secret of the powerful hold which this firm has on its thousands of customers scattered throughout the many Southern States. Probably no firm in the South enjoys the complete confidence of so large a number of dealers. It is this mutual understanding that is responsible for the large mail order business now being done by this firm, for a merchant can order in this way feeling confident that he will get exactly what he wants and that this confidence will never be misplaced.

As to the stocks carried, they could not be more complete, and the buyers are as familiar with every source of supply, both in America and foreign countries, as the salesmen are with the needs of their customers. As to its financial standing, this firm is as solid as the rock of Gibraltar, and can and does command the very lowest prices and discounts that cash and quantity will secure.

The accompanying cuts give a view into two different departments, and while they give some idea of the vast piles of goods carried in stock, they cannot show the attractive selection and the wonderful variety of the different lines.

Briefly summed up, Cowan, McClung & Company always has been the leading dry goods and notion house of Knoxville. It occupies that position today, and always will, if we can judge the future by the past.

OFFICERS		SALESMEN
SAM C. HOUSE, President	# House-Hasson Hardware Co.	C. S. Hasson—Tenn., Ga. and N. C.
C. S. HASSON, Vice-President	INCORPORATED	J. D. Hasson—Tenn. and N. C.
W. M. BONHAM, Secretary	EXCLUSIVELY WHOLESALE	C. A. Roth—Tenn. and Ky.
CHAS. M. MITCHELL, Treasurer	*Hardware, Stoves, Tinware, Etc.*	J. L. Phillips—N. C.
		J. F. Mary—Tenn.
		F. H. Rogan—Tenn., Ky. and Va.
		I. R. Smith—Tenn.
		Lee M. Ross—Tenn. and Ky.
		M. R. Calloway—Tenn., Va. and Ky.
		B. G. Clark—Tenn. and N. C.
		W. F. Roth—House Salesman.
		R. R. Roth—Office Salesman.

THE House-Hasson Hardware Company began business January 1, 1907. From the beginning they have adhered strictly to their policy of selling to merchants only, and are generally known as "**Knoxville's Exclusively Wholesale Hardware House.**"

They have a large and complete stock of goods, filling every available foot of floor space in an immense, well-located building and warehouse, which enables them to fill orders promptly and completely.

The growth of their business has been remarkable, and additional salesmen have been added from time to time, until now they have ten salesmen on the road, all of whom have increased their sales from the very first.

This organization is made up of men who have made Hardware their life work. Many of them have been actively engaged in it as salesmen, buyers, etc., for the fifth of a century. Notwithstanding this, they are today a group of young men in the most active period of life—the average age of the members of the company being less than forty years.

A liberal and progressive policy has marked the dealings of this company from the start, and the fact that its membership is composed of young and progressive men is evidence enough that they will continue to conduct their business in the same efficient, up-to-date manner.

With the addition of this large and enterprising hardware house, Knoxville has become more than ever the recognized hardware market for a large territory of which she is the geographical and railroad center.

A CORNER OF THE NOTION FLOOR

Brown, Payne, Deaver & Company

Wholesalers and Importers of Dry Goods, Notions and Furnishings

THE firm of Brown, Payne, Deaver & Company, Knoxville, began business ten years ago with sufficient capital to place it on an equal footing with older concerns. Its history has been one of steady growth. Its founders were young men, experienced buyers, good salesmen, and men of enterprise and push.

It would be hard at this time to find a better business in the South in the wholesale dry goods, notions and furnishings line than that done by this enterprising firm. They cover a territory embracing eight Southern States, and have on their books a large number of the best merchants in this territory. It is good business to get trade; it is better business to hold it against increasing competition. The great success of Brown, Payne, Deaver & Co. is attributable to the fact that they do both.

They do not claim to "handle the best goods in the world at the lowest prices," but come out boldly with the statement that each season they offer the dealer new goods in all grades that are obtained from the same sources of supply furnishing goods to the leading markets—goods bought for cash at such discounts that enable them to quote lower prices than houses in Eastern cities, where the expense of doing business is much greater, and to meet competition anywhere in the South. Furthermore, their goods are selected by buyers who know what will be in demand. It is their care in buying that makes selling easy for them and for their customers. Several years ago they began to speak of their lines as "Goods that won't stay on the shelves." This was suggested by continued rapid moving of stocks. It was true of the goods in their house, and, consequently true of the same goods when shown in the stores of the retailers.

The Southern merchant who handles dry goods, notions and furnishings cannot do a better thing than to accept the invitations, made by this house through their advertisements, to examine their lines and get their prices before placing orders. It is certainly worth while for a merchant to see for himself just why the goods sold by this concern move so fast, and why, as they claim, they seldom lose a customer whose trade is worth having. There are reasons for this—and good ones. If you visit Knoxville, which you should do, if you wish to look over the lines carried in the best market in the South, call on these enterprising people who are getting a larger share of the best Southern trade each year and holding on to it. If you don't come, see their salesmen. It pays to investigate, especially when a firm courts show-downs with competitors before experienced buyers.

This cut shows the home of BROYLES, McCLELLAN & LACKEY COMPANY, 306 Gay St., an alert and progressive house that has had much to do with the business improvement of this city. They are one of the largest manufacturers of Fertilizers, Harness and Saddles and wholesale and retail dealers in Seeds, Agricultural Implements, Machinery and Vehicles to be found in this section of the State. . . . .

IT would be difficult to do the above firm justice in a brief history, as few, if any of the firms composed of Knoxville men have made the advancements that they have since their organization, March 2nd, 1902. Their business has grown since that time to such an extent that their floor space has been doubled, to say nothing of their additional warehouse capacity. They manufacture their own Fertilizers, Harness and Saddles, carrying sufficient stock to supply their wholesale as well as retail trade throughout East Tennessee and adjoining States.

They also make a specialty of Field Seeds, Agricultural Implements, Harvesting Machinery, Saw Mills, Engines and Threshers and Vehicles of nearly every description. In Corn Planters and Cultivators the "Canton" is prominent. "Osborne" is their leader in Disc Harrows. They carry in stock a good line of "Russell" Engines and Saw Mills. They handle the well-known "Farmer's Favorite" Grain Drill. Their repository contains about sixty sample vehicles of as many different styles. This concern occupies a five story and basement building 36 x 160, aggregating about 25,000 feet, and in addition to this they have warehouses on the Southern Railway, 503 East Jackson Ave., and 130 West Jackson Ave., where their heavy machinery and fertilizer are stored. Their business method of purchasing their goods in car load lots has enabled them to offer moderate prices to the trade.

Special attention is devoted to their mail-order department, and through this medium they are distributing their goods well over the Southern States.

THE HORSE-SHOE IS THE ONLY TRADE-MARK THAT SPELLS

THE HORSE-SHOE STANDS AS A MERIT MARK FOR

HORSE-SHOE BRAND SHOES

ALWAYS WHEN BUYING SHOES
LOOK FOR THE MERIT MARK

MEN'S SPECIALTIES
THAT CREATE
BUSINESS:

"The Arnold"
"Golden Rule"
"Forest King"
"Admiral Togo"

WOMEN'S
SPECIALTIES THAT
ATTRACT TRADE:

"American Queen"
"Reigning Queen"
"The Raven"
"Shamrock"

Our Spring Line of Horse-Shoe Brand Shoes, now on the road, excels all previous offerings in artistic merit. The new line, as a whole, embodies all of the latest models and most popular leathers. It offers careful buyers an exceptional opportunity to secure for their trade the best quality, the highest grade of material and workmanship at prices we know are right. The line that grows fastest must truly have a reason. **74 % gain on road sales for September, first month with new line, prove our claims**

Greater Knoxville's Greater Shoes

ARNOLD, HENEGAR, DOYLE & COMPANY

GILLESPIE, SHIELDS & CO., MANUFACTURERS OF "SHIELD BRAND" CLOTHING

A LITTLE less than nine years ago Gillespie Shields & Co., now the largest manufacturers and wholesalers of clothing south of Baltimore, started in business with only two salesmen and a very small house force.

Since that time their business has rapidly grown each year, until today they travel twenty-one salesmen, which is the largest sales force covering the Southern States in the interest of any one clothing house, with a proportionately increased house force.

The phenomenal growth of their business is due in a large measure to their having adopted improved methods of buying, manufacturing and selling clothing.

Realizing the advantages of buying piece goods in lishing same in the minds of the wearers as being dependable.

They accordingly adopted a shield and the words "Shield Brand" as their trade-mark, and began advertising same, which they afterwards registered. The advertising proved of great value to the retail merchants, inasmuch as it increased their sales on "Shield Brand" clothing.

As a result of such progressiveness and efforts on the part of this firm "Shield Brand" has become the largest and only universally distributed popular priced clothing sold from any market in the Southern States.

This firm has one of the largest and best equipped advertising departments to be found in the South, and

large quantities direct from the largest mills for spot cash, their buyers entered the piece goods market accordingly, having previously arranged for turning out the made-up garments under their own supervision, incorporating their own ideas and knowledge of the needs of the Southern trade into the suits.

They also adopted the net price plan in connection with the sale of their clothing, giving the retail merchants the lowest possible price to be had on dependable garments, thus placing themselves on record as being the pioneers in the South of the net cash clothing business.

These methods have been maintained and improved from time to time and they finally conceived and adopted the idea of advertising a popular priced line of clothing in behalf of the retail merchants for the purpose of estab-

spends a large amount of money each year for the purpose of assisting their many customers to dispose of "Shield Brand" clothing profitably.

Their improved methods of buying, manufacturing and selling has made "Shield Brand" clothing an almost irresistible article of merchandise to the retail merchants of the South, while their effective advertising renders same almost indispensable.

This firm was first to adopt the net price plan in connection with the sale of ready-made clothing; first to incorporate high art features; first to advertise a popular priced line of clothing, and first to attach retail price to suits, and as a result of such progressiveness have built up the largest clothing business in the South.

SHIELD BRAND CLOTHING SALESMEN

THE LARGEST CORPS OF SALESMEN TRAVELING SOUTHERN STATES IN THE INTEREST OF ANY ONE CLOTHING HOUSE.

1—Z. T. GODWIN, JR., Eastern North Carolina and Virginia.
2—D. T. VESTAL, Virginia and North Carolina.
3—S. O. MANARD, House Salesman.
4—R. R. CAIRNS, Southern Mississippi.
5—W. W. PORTER, East Tennessee and Western North Carolina.
6—O. F. O'DANIEL, Western Tennessee.
7—CHARLES WEST, Southern Georgia and Florida.
8—L. A. CROOM, Southern Arkansas.
9—F. P. HAGER, Western and Central Kentucky.
10—C. H. WHITNER, Northern Georgia.
11—P. A. KIDD, Tennessee and Kentucky.
12—R. W. SOWERS, Sales and Advertising Manager.
13—B. G. PETERS, Eastern Kentucky.
14—W. L. MORGAN, Northern Mississippi.
15—L. J. PETERS, City Salesman.
16—R. H. McNUTT, Southern Alabama.
17—A. W. BOWDEN, Middle Tennessee.
18—F. R. NEAL, Georgia and Alabama.
19—G. M. HALL, Northern Alabama.
20—J. L. MITCHELL, North and South Carolina.
21—W. H. PETERS, Oklahoma and Indian Territory.
22—C. L. PARROTT, South Carolina and Georgia.
23—W. L. OWEN, Northern Arkansas.
24—R. D. RODGERS, Tennessee and Alabama.

GILLESPIE, SHIELDS & CO.

Manufacturers "Shield Brand" Clothing.

KNOXVILLE, TENNESSEE

Chapman's WHITE LION, for more than a quarter of a century a familiar figure at 214 South Gay Street

Every Item Manufactured, Distributed, Packed or Sold by the Chapman Drug Company is GUARANTEED under the National Pure Food and Drug Act Guarantee 223

The White Lion Label is older, and better, than the National Pure Food and Drug Act, for it Guarantees superior excellence and strength, as well as purity

CHAPMAN'S WHITE LION BRAND

Of Bottled and Package Drugs Embodies the Highest Degree of Purity, Strength and Excellence

¶The White Lion Label on any bottle or package of drugs, flavoring extracts or sundry specials, *guarantees* the contents to be absolutely pure, of standard strength and supreme excellence.

¶*Druggists and Dealers* who desire to build up a reputation for handling *the best*, and at the same time build up the *biggest* business in these lines, must handle *White Lion* brand. *Consumers* who want the best, can get it by *demanding White Lion Brand*.

We are Sole Distributors for the Famous *Royal Amber* Ginger Ale

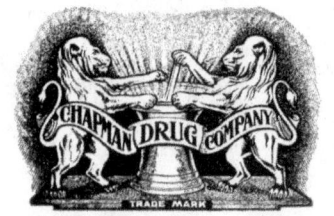

This is the WHITE LION LABEL

CHAPMAN
DRUG COMPANY

Successors to the Chapman, White, Lyons Company
ESTABLISHED 1881 --- INCORPORATED 1907

KNOXVILLE, TENNESSEE

This is the WHITE LION LABEL

A Revolution in Gas Lighting.

..... The ..... Knoxville Gas Company

The Knoxville Gas Company has kept pace with the rapid progress of the city, and not only meets the wants of its customers, but also trys to anticipate them wherever possible. Their network of feeder pipes supplies gas to many of the adjoining suburbs, as well as the city proper.

Realizing the enormous value a properly managed gas company is to its city and its customers, the company strives to give the best possible service, and also operates a special department to secure the most efficient gas appliances made for the customers of the company.

Appreciation of our efforts is shown by the public in utilizing gas for over 500 different purposes, each one having its special value from the standpoint of convenience, cleanliness, economy or comfort.

Our constant effort is, and will be, to make The Knoxville Gas Company the most popular of public corporations and to boost for Knoxville, the City of Progress.

Powers Little & Company

LIBERAL TERMS	CLOSEST PRICES
FACTORY 131-133 BLEEKER STREET NEW YORK	SALES OFFICE 124 JACKSON AVE. KNOXVILLE, TENN.
CLOSEST PRICES	LIBERAL TERMS

MANUFACTURERS OF
.........THE FAMOUS.........

"KNOX BRAND CLOTHING"

MEDIUM GRADE

FOR MEN, YOUTHS, BOYS

Unequaled In Fit, Finish, Fabric

Garments sold by us are made by us. We buy the material direct from the mills. We create styles to please the Southern trade. We make up and finish suits as ordered by our customers. KNOX BRAND CLOTHING is matchless in style, unequaled at the price, and sells fast at good profit.

KNOX BRAND Clothing gives complete satisfaction to dealer and wearer.

Twenty Years of Success in Selling to Southern Merchants.

The firm of POWERS, LITTLE & COMPANY has been selling clothing to Southern merchants for TWENTY YEARS. During that time its business has grown from small proportions until today it is one of the foremost clothing concerns of the South.

Its success, in a large measure, is due to the fact that the members of the firm have constantly given their personal attention to its conduct. They have kept in close touch with the needs of their customers, and have met and often anticipated the wants of the Southern trade. LIBERAL TERMS, FAIR TREATMENT, THE BEST STYLES AND THE BEST VALUES are the three cardinal principles upon which this business has been built and by which its patronage is firmly secured. They greatly appreciate and highly prize the patronage given them by their customers, and solicit a continuance of the same.

SPENCE TRUNK & LEATHER GOODS COMPANY

309-311 GAY STREET, KNOXVILLE, TENNESSEE

LARGEST LEATHER GOODS STORE IN THE SOUTH

BAGS, KNIVES, SUIT CASES, TOILET SETS, DOG COLLARS, MANICURE SETS. . . . . . .

LEGGINS, UMBRELLAS, BILL BOOKS, CUFF BOXES, MUSIC ROLLS, DRINKING CUPS. . .

. . . . AGENTS FOR . . . .

REGAL SHOES AT $3.50 AND $4.00
FOR
MEN AND WOMEN

Our Line is as Complete as Found in Any Regal Store

CHILDREN'S SHOES A SPECIALTY

Links in the Chain of a Successful Career

THE business career of Hon. Peter Kern, president and founder of the Peter Kern Co., Inc., furnishes an example of what pluck, energy and faithful application can accomplish. Born at Zwingeberg, Hesse Darmstatt, a village near Heidelburg, Germany, Oct. 31, 1835, he early conceived the idea of making the best of his opportunity.

Hearing of America, he decided to cast his lot here. A youth of eighteen and a half summers, with little more than sufficient to pay his passage to New York, he bravely faced the future.

With undaunted self-confidence and a desire to work his way to the top, naturally apt and industrious, he soon made a place for himself.

Landing in New York in the spring of 1854, after a rough voyage of some thirty-one days, "a stranger in a strange land," he soon secured employment at his trade at small wages and board.

The winter was unusually cold, so the following fall he sailed for Charleston, spending the winter there. The following summer yellow fever broke out in Charleston and Mr. Kern went North to Philadelphia. In the fall of 1857 Mr. Kern took passage to Savannah.

Anxious to learn the language of the land of his adoption, he soon came to the conclusion that he must give up the companionship of those of his own language and cast his lot with the American-speaking people.

The opportunity soon presented itself. A gentleman was in search of a shoemaker to take to Tallahassee, Fla. Mr. Kern was offered the position, which he accepted.

From Tallahassee Mr. Kern went to Valdosta, Ga., thence to Thompson, Ga., where he made friends, was well thought of and prospered.

At the break'ng out of the war Mr. Kern went to the front with the young men of the community to fight for the cause of his friends.

Being wounded at the battle of McDowell, he was sent to the rear. His wound healing slowly, he was allowed a furlough to go South, and later was ordered back to Richmond.

On his way to the front Mr. Kern stopped over at Knoxville, Tenn., to see friends. A few days later Gen. Burnside took possession of Knoxville, blocking the way to Richmond.

Soon after coming to Knoxville Mr. Kern met a young German, a baker by trade, and they decided to go into the baking business. Though not a baker, Mr. Kern's rare business instincts and keen judgment soon asserted themselves in making success of seeming failure. Soon coming to the conclusion that the business was too small for two, he approached his partner with a proposition to buy or sell, and Mr. Kern bought out his partner.

From this humble beginning Mr. Kern built up one of the leading industries of the city—the pride of the citizens, and a monument to his credit.

Always a firm believer in the future of Knoxville, Mr. Kern was always ready to give time, as well as means, to forward the best interests of the city, feeling that Knoxville's interest was Kern's interests, that his business would grow as the city grew.

As an expression of appreciation, the citizens elected Mr. Kern to the Board of Aldermen, the Board of Public Works and Mayor of the city, the city receiving a sound, clean business administration.

The Peter Kern Co., Incorporated, is a close corporation, stock being held by the sons and daughters of Mr. Kern, of which there are ten.

The company employs from eighty to one hundred people, manufacturing Candies, Cakes, Bread, Ice Cream, etc., doing a general wholesale and retail business, soliciting Southern trade, ever endeavoring to make only the purest goods at reasonable prices, feeling that merit wins in the long run, and that there is a ready market for quality.

The firm solicits your trade and it will ever endeavor to live up to the high standard set by the founder and president of the company.

THE IMPORTANCE OF KNOXVILLE AS A COAL CENTER

BY E. C. MAHAN

IT requires only a glance at the map by any one familiar with the coal-producing section and the coal-consuming section of the Southeast to see that Knoxville occupies the logical location as the coal-distributing point of this great territory. It, in fact, bears the same relation to the coal-producing and consuming fields of the Southeast as is occupied by the neck of an hour glass. On the one side are the great coal fields embracing the Coal Creek, Oliver Springs, Jellico, Middlesboro, Cumberland Valley and Laurel County fields, comprising very largely the entire coal fields of Eastern Tennessee and Kentucky, with the railroads from all these fields converging at Knoxville. On the other side is the great coal-consuming territory of the Southeast, with the railroads, in turn, diverging from Knoxville and carrying this coal to their markets.

Men in the coal business have not been slow in appreciating Knoxville's great natural advantages as a distributing point, and from the inception of mining in these fields, it has occupied a leading position as a coal-distributing the domestic coals produced that Knoxville enjoys the distinction of being the distributing point of more strictly high-grade bituminous domestic coal than any other city in the United States. There are other places where much more domestic coal is marketed, but it is not of the same quality as that in the coal measures embraced in the Jellico field. In no other section of the country is there so much high-grade bituminous coal produced in one field as there is in the Jellico field. This coal without doubt enjoys a wider market than any other bituminous coal produced in this country. It is marketed all the way from Florida to the Northwestern States.

The especially encouraging feature that Knoxville enjoys as a coal-distributing center, is that the development of the great fields that contribute to her position, is as yet only begun. Within one year from the present time there will be no less than twenty-five new mines in this territory that will be contributing their proportion to the maintenance of Knoxville as a coal center. New railroads are being con-

VIEW SHOWING AN INCLINE IN OPERATION AT ONE OF THE COAL MINES NEAR KNOXVILLE

center in the South, and holds the same position today to an even larger extent.

Of the coal fields mentioned above, the Coal Creek, Oliver Springs and Middlesboro fields, which are located in Tennessee, produce almost entirely steam coal. The Cumberland Valley and Laurel County sections, which are located in Kentucky, are largely producers of steam coal, but ship probably twenty-five per cent of their output for domestic purposes. The Jellico field, which, in its full sense, embraces a territory of about forty square miles, and is about evenly divided by the Kentucky-Tennessee State line, produces domestic coal entirely, with the exception of about one-third of the output, consisting of screenings, which is sold principally for steam purposes.

The steam coals produced in this section enjoy an enviable reputation and constitute at least three-fourths of the volume of coal business. It is, however, on account of structed each year, reaching back further and further into the hitherto undeveloped territory, and even under the most favorable conditions it will be not less than twenty-five years yet before the coal territory of which Knoxville is the logical distributing center will have reached its maximum output.

While the fields mentioned above furnish decidedly the largest proportion of coal, of which Knoxville is the distributing point, there is in addition a large amount of coal from the other coal fields of Tennessee, as well as from the Virginia fields, that is placed on the market from this point. Already there are in Knoxville forty coal companies, doing approximately an annual business of ten million dollars. It would not seem to be an extravagant statement by any means to say that this business would be doubled within the next ten years, and that Knoxville is destined to command a more important position as a coal center with each passing year.

A. GATLIFF, President T. B. MAHAN, Vice President

E. C. MAHAN, General Manager Sales Department

N. B. PERKINS, General Manager Mining Department

SOUTHERN COAL & COKE COMPANY

INCORPORATED

Lexington, Ky.   Atlanta, Ga.   Winston=Salem, N. C.

GENERAL OFFICES:

KNOXVILLE - - - - TENNESSEE

Mines on L. & N., Southern and N. & W. Railroads

Largest Producers and Shippers of Strictly High Grade Coal in the South

Daily Capacity of Mines

By October 1908

5000 TONS

JELLICO   BLUE GEM   REGAL BLOCK   POCAHONTAS

Knoxville Has In

The Phonograph Store

At 421 Gay Street

The largest retail talking machine house in the United States

It carries a stock of over 80,000 records

More than 3,000 Knoxvillians have purchased phonographs

at this store in the past three years

W. N. SMITH

MANUFACTURER
WHOLESALE   RETAIL

...Furniture...

Carpets

Pianos

Organs

WRITE FOR

Smith's Illustrated Catalog

IT'S FREE

SALESROOM

302 Gay Street

Knoxville - - Tennessee

MEN'S HATS　　　　　　　　*McCulley*　　　　　　　　MILLINERY

Hat Company

MANUFACTURERS – JOBBERS

In Millinery The Largest Manufacturers and Trimmers in the South.

We invite the Milliners of Tennessee, Alabama, Mississippi, Georgia, North Carolina, Virginia. West Virginia and Kentucky to come to Knoxville and make our store their headquarters, where they will be given facilities for copying our imported pattern hats with one of our expert milliners at their disposal. We give our customers the fullest information concerning advance styles and assist them in every way possible.

McCulley's Matchless Specials in Men's Hats

"McCulley," $24.00　　　"Diamond," $18.00　　　"Victory," . . . $12.00
"Electric," $24.00　　　"Perfection," $12.00　　　"American Beauty," $9.00

McCulley's Men's Hats sell at sight to the trade and to their trade.
We carry a mammoth stock and the widest variety of styles.

Knoxville . . . . . *Tennessee*

THE THIRD NATIONAL BANK

The Third National Bank of Knoxville, Tenn., was organized in March, 1887. The first officers were General R. N. Hood, President; R. P. Gettys, Vice President; J. A. McKeldin, Cashier; H. B. Branner, Assistant Cashier.

Through all its history it has been known as the Business Man's Bank, ever ready to lend a helping hand to legitimate business enterprises, to foster and encourage manufactures, and to assist in every proper way in the upbuilding and commercial life of Knoxville; and to-day is recognized as one of the leading financial institutions of the South, and a potent factor in the banking world of this section.

The present management is aggressive and up-to-date. The officers are H. B. Branner, President; E. E. McMillan, Vice President; and C. M. Cooley, Cashier.

The progress of the bank has been characterized by steady growth, not only in its deposits, but in its surplus, and to-day it stands as the only bank in Knoxville having a surplus actually earned---none having been paid in by its stockholders. It has a capital of $200,000, a surplus fund of $112,000 and deposits that average around one and one quarter million dollars.

The East Tennessee National Bank

THE East Tennessee National Bank of Knoxville was organized in August, 1872, with a paid-in capital of $100,000. The first officers were R. C. Jackson, president; F. H. McClung, vice-president; and W. B. French, cashier. Mr. French resigned in 1873 and was succeeded by J. W. Lillard.

In January, 1874, the capital stock of the bank was increased to $150,000, and reduced to $100,000 in 1877. J. W. Lillard resigned as cashier in February, 1878. In January, 1879, Joseph Jaques was elected president and R. C. Jackson cashier. W. W. Woodruff was elected vice-president in January, 1882, and one year later Joseph Jaques resigned as president and was succeeded by R. C. Jackson. J. L. Glover was elected cashier in July, 1883. In July of that year R. S. Payne was elected to succeed W. W. Woodruff, who resigned as vice-president. J. L. Glover died in August, 1883, and F. L. Fisher was elected cashier. R. C. Jackson resigned in April, 1884, and R. S. Payne was elected president and E. J. Sanford vice-president. The capital stock was increased to $175,000 in April, 1887. B. R. Strong succeeded R. S. Payne, resigned as president, March, 1892. In May, 1894, Mr. Strong resigned and F. L. Fisher was elected president and S. V. Carter cashier. F. L. Fisher and S. V. Carter have served as president and cashier continuously to the present time. In May, 1904, the capital was increased to $200,000, and in January, 1906, to $400,000.

The business of the bank has grown steadily from the beginning to the present time. The total deposits in March, 1873, were $229,066.19. On August 22, 1907, the total deposits were $2,566,056.80.

The East Tennessee National Bank has never passed a dividend, and since its organization has paid sixty-eight semi-annual dividends.

The following is a copy of the last published statement to the Controller, issued August 22, 1907:

UNITED STATES DEPOSITORY

Statement of the condition of the bank at close of business Aug. 22, 1907.

RESOURCES		LIABILITIES	
Loans, discounts, securities,	$1,970,830.42	Capital Stock,	$400,000.00
Overdrafts,	1,867.63	Surplus Fund and Profits (net),	166,243.57
United States Bonds,	450,000.00	Circulation,	400,000.00
Premiums paid on U. S. Bonds,	none	Deposits,	2,566,056.80
Banking House,	65,000.00		
Due from Reserve Agents, $378,683.43			
Due from Banks, 441,689.43			
Due from U. S. Treasurer, 20,000.00			
Cash, 204,229.59	1,044,602.32		
	$3,532,300.37		$3,532,300.37

WE SOLICIT YOUR BUSINESS.
SAFETY DEPOSIT BOXES FOR RENT.   NEW STEEL VAULTS—FIRE AND BURGLAR PROOF.

FRANK J. CALLAN   Established 1871

DESIGNER AND MAKER OF MEN'S CLOTHES
S. W. COR. GAY AND CHURCH STREETS.

GAY STREET, NEXT TO STAUB'S THEATRE

YOU GO TO   **"The Colonial"**   EUROPEAN

Knoxville's Newest and Best Hotel

STRICTLY MODERN.

FIREPROOF,
EQUIPPED
THROUGHOUT
WITH AUTOMATIC
SPRINKLERS

A COZY, CLUB-LIKE
HOTEL.
YOU'LL LIKE IT.

ROOM RATES:
WITH BATH
$1.50 AND A FEW
AT $2.00
WITHOUT
BATH
$1.00

ONE OF THE
NICEST
HOTELS IN THE
SOUTH

Seventy-five Rooms, Forty with Luxurious Tiled Bath

CAFE SERVICE UNEXCELLED. PRICES REASONABLE

M. M. NEWCOMER & CO.

Knoxville's Department Store

FRONT VIEW NEW JEWELRY STORE OF LUCAS THE "HUSTLER"

Knoxville's Most Enterprising and Up-to-Date Jeweler

BUY IT OF

Lucas The "Hustler"

AND

BANK THE DIFFERENCE

INTERIOR VIEW NEW JEWELRY STORE OF LUCAS THE "HUSTLER"

KUHLMAN'S
Modern Cut-Rate Drug Stores

STORE No. 1, 301 GAY STREET

Most complete and extensive stocks of Drugs, Patent Medicines, Pharmaceuticals and sundries in the South :: :: :: :: ::

Prescription service unexcelled :: :: ::

Sole Agents for the famous Rexall Remedies :: :: ::

STORE No. 3, 312 W. CLINCH

All Popular Cigars at Cut Prices. Agents for the National Cigar Stand Brands.
TWO MODERN FOUNTAINS ALWAYS BUSY
Agents for Huyler's, Lowney's, Fenway Fine Candies, and Belle Mead Sweets.

South Knoxville Macadam Co., under the management of W. R. Jones

JNO. G. DUNCAN CO.
308 W. JACKSON AVE.
KNOXVILLE   TENNESSEE

DEALERS IN

Engines   Boilers
Saw Mills
Wood-Working
Machinery

NEW AND
SECOND HAND

Old Phone 1442
New   "   1368

STEAMER J. L. DYKES

Operating between Knoxville and Chattanooga, and by transferring at Chattanooga makes through line to Decatur, Ala. Arrive at Knoxville Thursdays. Leave Fridays at 6:30 P. M. Reaches Chattanooga Tuesdays, A. M. Leaves Chattanooga Wednesdays at 10 A. M. Freight and passenger boat leaves Chattanooga Saturday 6 P. M. Operated and managed by sole owner, Mr. J. L. Dykes, who has had seventeen years experience in the steamboat business. All passengers are given courteous attention. Goods handled with care. Temperance prevails over all.

THE NAME OF BLAUFELD . . . .

Is like a trade-mark on the back of a silver plate. It means Segars well made, of the Best Tobacco, by Cuban craftsmen faithful to traditional art of perfect cigar making, well kept in our Segar Vaults to maturity, in many sizes of the following brands: "Chas. the Great," "Mi Eleceion," "Henry Fourth," "Bouquet de Trujello," "El Sidello," and "Flor de Mendel," besides various other well known brands . . . .

J. BLAUFELD, 526 Gay St., Knoxville, Tenn.

ORGANIZED 1889   INCORPORATED 1894

The Fair Foundry Co.

Stoves and General Foundry Business

J. E. FAIR, Prest., Treas. & Mgr.   WM. P. RICHARDS, Vice-President   J. W. HISCOCK, Secretary

Pope-Waverley Automobiles

Here you see, in a setting quite befitting its stylish, graceful lines and superb finish, the handsomest, most stylish and luxurious carriage in all motordom. It is the Model 67, Victoria Phaeton.

RODGERS & CO.
710 GAY ST.

COTTAGE HOME
DAIRY GARDENS

W. R. TEEPELL
Knoxville, Tenn.
ROUTE 6

1. First Location, 1865.
2. Second Location, 1868-75.
3. Present Building.
4. Battery of Ovens. (AP. 20,000 loaves a day)
5. Ice Cream Parlors.
6. Retail Store Room.

"The Business Grew, the Building Didn't. Mighty Oaks From Little Acorns Grow."

A Story in Picture

Sanford, Chamberlain & Albers Company...

WHOLESALE AND MANUFACTURING DRUGGISTS

THIS oldest and leading drug house of Knoxville was established in 1864, just previous to the close of the Civil War, and has continued the drug business continually since that time. Its long and successful life speaks well for its methods of fair dealing and the character, quality, variety and completeness of its large stock. There is probably no business house in the entire South better or more favorably known than that of Sanford, Chamberlain & Albers Co. This concern is the owner and proprietor of Dr. Hart's Family Medicines—Relief, Symphyx, etc. Besides the full line of Drugs, Chemicals and Patent Medicines carried on, one department is devoted to the sale of Lubricating Oils of great variety; also the handling of Cement, both native and Portland, Paints, Oils, etc.

The officers of the company are A. J. Albers, president; A. F. Sanford, vice-president; Wm. P. Chamberlain, secretary and treasurer. Location in the center of the business district—No. 430 Gay Street.

NEW PHONE 857   OLD PHONE 2192

M. L. WOLF

AUTOMOBILE GARAGE AND REPAIR SHOP

SAFE, KEY AND LOCK WORK A SPECIALTY

General Machine Work.   710 GAY ST.

ESTABLISHED 1890   NEW PHONE 572

B. B. DALLAS

MANUFACTURER OF

Boilers, Smoke Stacks, Breechings, Tanks

GENERAL BOILER REPAIRING

201 JACKSON AVE.   KNOXVILLE, TENN.

VIEWS FROM THE SOUTHERN COAL & COKE COMPANY AND SOME OF ITS ASSOCIATED MINES

Regal FULL HIP LONG WAIST Pants

mean more to you than any other makes, because they bring you clear profit. . . .

For instance, you can get as much for a **Regal** $21.00 article as you can for the other fellow's $24.00 goods. And you supply your customer with more satisfaction besides. . . . .

MAKE US PROVE IT

THE REGAL MFG. CO.
OF KNOXVILLE
SOLE MAKERS AND DISTRIBUTORS

W.W. WOODRUFF HARDWARE CO. KNOXVILLE, TENN.

AGENTS FOR

Oliver Chilled Plows

Heath & Milligan Prepared Paints

Railway White Lead

Spalding Athletic Goods

Parker and Ithaca Shot Guns

Quick Meal Ranges

Jewel Heaters

DEALERS IN ALL KINDS OF HARDWARE

KNOXVILLE WATER COMPANY

One of the most progressive enterprises of the city is the Knoxville Water Co., whose plant embraces 120 miles of mains and a pumping station, filtration plant and laboratory equipped with the latest facilities for furnishing consumers with the best possible product. Its present pumping capacity is 9,000,000 gallons per day, and the company is now installing an additional 10,000,000 gallon pump of the most modern type, thereby assuring the city an ample and reliable water supply. This the citizens of Knoxville appreciate, and they feel that because of the efforts of the management of the Knoxville Water Company no city in the country is supplied with a better and purer product.

FILTERING PLANT AND STAND PIPE OF THE KNOXVILLE WATER COMPANY

HOTEL IMPERIAL
R. W. FARR, Manager
KNOXVILLE, TENNESSEE

KNOXVILLE'S LEADING HOTEL

William J. Oliver
GENERAL CONTRACTOR   KNOXVILLE, TENN.
PARTNERS AND BUSINESS ASSOCIATES

L. E. WOOTEN
Traveling Engineer, Knoxville.

J. L. BOWLES, JR.
Chief Clerk

H. L. PIKE
Auditor

L. C. GUNTER
General Manager W. J. Oliver Construction Co. and Vice President The Wm. J. Oliver Mfg. Co.

WILLIAM J. OLIVER

W. A. SEYMOUR
Chief Engineer, Wm. J. Oliver and Wm. J. Oliver Construction Co.

B. R. STOUT
Purchasing Agent, Knoxville

R. L. SITES
Assistant to President, The Wm. J. Oliver Mfg. Co.,, Knoxville

FRED A. PECKHAM
General Sales Agent The Wm. J. Oliver Mfg. Co., New York and Chicago.

BUSINESS ASSOCIATES OF WM. J. OLIVER

R. E. OLIVER
Oliver Bros. & Callaway, Winfield, Tenn.

R. B. OLIVER
R. B. Oliver, Inc., Statesboro, Ga.

ROBERT RUSSELL
Russell & Oliver
Lynchburg, Virginia.

H. H. THRASHER
H. H. Thrasher & Company, Knoxville.

CHAS. YANDELL
Chas. Yandell Co., Statesboro, Ga.

C. J. McKINNEY
McKinney & Oliver, Knoxville and
New Orleans.

W. E. MILLS
President James Supply Co.
Chattanooga.

R. H. WALKER
President T. G. Lamar-Kaolin Co.,
Langley, S. C.

O. O. SNYDER
O. O. Snyder & Co., Grain Elevator and
Lumber and General Merchandise,
Pryor Creek, I. T.

THOS. PRUDEN
Pruden Coal Co., Knoxville.

R. F. RIVINAC
R. F. Rivinac & Co., Charlotte, N. C.

H. C. McCRARY
H. C. McCrary & Co., Knoxville.

O. G. HUFF
O. G. Huff Lumber Co., South Bend, Ind.

GASTON O'BRIEN
Gaston O'Brien & Co., Knoxville.

T. P. ROBERTS
Superintendent The Wm. J. Oliver Mfg.
Co., Knoxville.

C. S. McMANUS
President Sterling Coal Co. and Winona
Coal Co., Middlesboro, Ky.

The Oliver Cars...

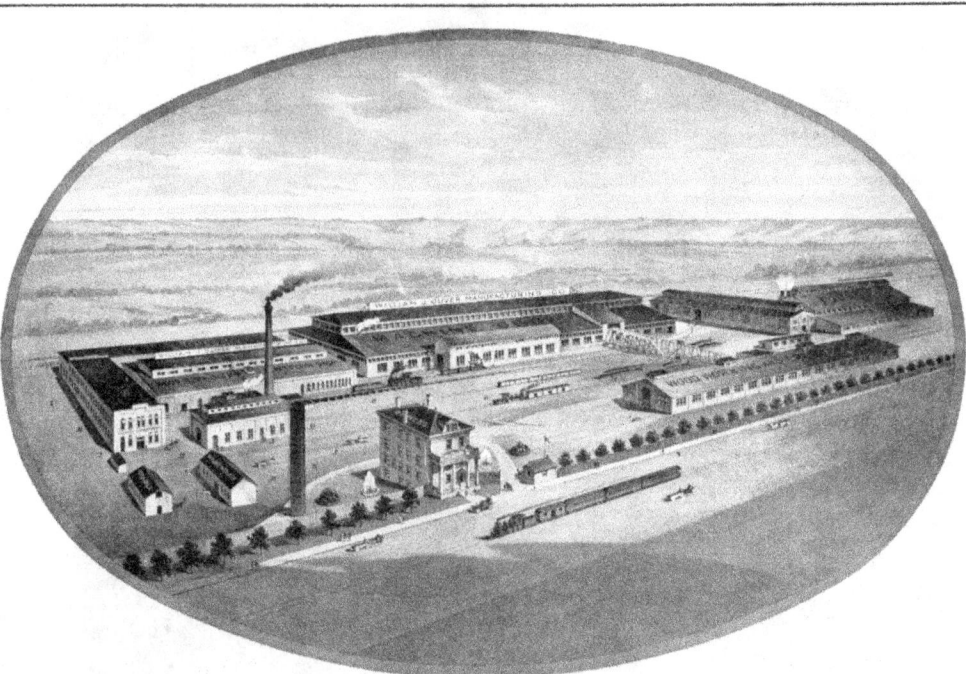

Manufacturers of Complete Contractors' and Mine Cars and Supplies. . . . .

Dump Cars from 1 yard to 20 Yards Capacity, both Steel and Wood. . . .

An up-to-date foundry operated in conjunction with our plant places us in position to at all times fill orders promptly and at minimum cost. . . . . . .

Castings and Foundry Supplies of Every Description.

The accompanying cut is that of a 12-yard OLIVER Dump Car, similar in design to the lot of 500 (all steel) dump cars recently sold to the United States Government for use at the Isthmus to be used in connection with the construction of the canal. . . . . . .

UPRIGHT POSITION

The awarding of the contract to the OLIVER type of car by the Government is sufficient guarantee that they are the best on the market, as they were sold in competition with every known dump car. . . .

We also manufacture screens, tipples, drums, marble finishing machinery and a full line of mechanical appliances of all kinds. . . .

Correspondence Solicited.

The Wm. J. Oliver Manufacturing Co.
DALE AVENUE

DUMPED POSITION

THE PROCTER COAL COMPANY,-INC.

Mining Operations, JELLICO, TENN. General Sales Department, KNOXVILLE, TENN.

PRODUCERS AND SHIPPERS OF

The only Red Ash and Indian Mountain
JELLICO COAL

Of all the coal companies in this section **THE PROCTER COAL COMPANY** is the largest producer and the most widely known.

The quality of the coal produced by it is universally recognized as the standard and as material evidence of the merit of its product, the *Red Ash* and *Indian Mountain* Jellico coal produced and sold exclusively by this Company, commands preference in every market in the South.

This is the only company in the Jellico district that is directly accessible to both the Southern and Louisville & Nashville Railways, and having the advantage of the transportation facilities of both lines.

The property of the Company embraces 14,000 acres of Jellico Coal Lands in the heart of the Jellico district, only about seven hundred of which have been exhausted. Five miles of standard guage railway under its direct control and operation. Four mines in actual operation with modern equipment and all the facilities necessary for the proper handling of its large output.

So great is the demand for this Copany's coal that the present equipment, already the largest and most extensive in the State, is being supplemented with a giant electrical plant that will furnish power from a central point to all portions of the large property and supply an increased out-put of coal that will provide for all demands.

The up-to-date and liberal business methods employed in the conduct of its affairs, together with its high class product has brought the success it deserves and made it the leading coal company of the South.

No connection nor association with OIL TRUST **Tennessee Oil Co.** **Independent Oil Co.**

KNOXVILLE, TENN.

Refiners and Manufacturers of all grades Lubricating and Lamp Oils from Premium Pennsylvania Crude.

Our Oils are absolutely free from Tar.

Sole Manufacturers SOLINE Lamp Oil.

Brilliant burner, oderless and smokeless. The only first class burning oil sold in the South.

New 'Phone 837 **Old 'Phone 323**

The above is a fair representation of our work
DAVID GETAZ, SON AND COMPANY, BUILDERS
Office Van Deventer Bldg.   Knoxville, Tennessee

W. H. BURK, C. E.

507 VAN DEVENTER BUILDING   KNOXVILLE, TENNESSEE

DESIGN and CONSTRUCTION
OF
STEEL and REINFORCED CONCRETE STRUCTURES,
FOUNDATIONS :: :: :: INDUSTRIAL BUILDINGS

KNOXVILLE BRICK COMPANY

VIEW OF WORKS, SHOWING SIX OF THEIR NINE KILNS

Dry Pressed Front and Ornamental and Common Building Brick

WORKS: Powell Sta., Tenn.   OFFICE: Empire Bldg., Knoxville, Tenn.

ESTABLISHED 1889

Hall & Donahue Coffin Company

THE Hall & Donahue Coffin Company has a patent Casket that will make easy work for the undertaker, and, it is believed, will revolutionize the casket handle business. This patent covers a casket with steel sides and the handle, which is elegant and the strongest one yet made, is a protusion of the solid steel of the solid side of the casket. The casket can be finished in varnish or cloth. The tacking on of the name plate makes it ready for use.

The Hall & Donahue Coffin Company have had for years a well-earned reputation for nice finish and good designs. They keep in stock Casket Hardware, Burial Robes, Linings, Embalming Fluids, and all Undertaking Supplies.

The location of their factory, near the Southern Depot, and their office, which is open day and night, next door to Western Union Telegraph Office, makes it possible for them to ship hurry orders on less notice than any concern in existence.

Give them a trial and they will hold your trade.

W. J. SAVAGE   CHAS. M. FUNCK

ESTABLISHED 1885

W. J. SAVAGE & CO.

Engineers
Founders
AND
Machinists

DEALERS IN
Mill
Supplies
Elevators
Hand or Power

MANUFACTURERS OF

Roller Flour Mill and Marble Mill Machinery

MILL ROLLS, GROUND AND CORRUGATED

===== AGENTS FOR =====

Dodge Mfg. Co.'s Transmission Machinery.

ALSO JOBBING AND REPAIR WORK

BOTH PHONES 1436

OFFICE AND WORKS
K. & A. R. R. and Clinch St.

A. F. SANDFORD, Manager   E. W. OGDEN, Secretary

Established 1839. Daily, Sunday and Week Editions

The Journal and Tribune

Is the only Morning and Sunday Paper in Knoxville and the Leader in News, Circulation and Advertising :: :: ::

CIRCULATION:

Double	*Twenty Times*	*Fifty Per Cent.*
Out of town Circulation	Knox County Rural Delivery Circulation	Larger City Circulation

THAN ANY OTHER KNOXVILLE PAPER

ADVERTISING:

The field covered by the *Journal and Tribune* is rich in opportunities for live advertisers. It covers not only the local field but all of the East Tennessee section. Both general and local advertisers secure big results. :: :: :: :: ::

NEWS:

With the Associated Press, local staff and corps of live correspondents, the *Journal and Tribune* is one of the newsiest, brightest and best papers for news in the entire South. Advertising and circulation rates on application.

In Knoxville and East Tennessee Nearly Everybody Reads

The Knoxville Sentinel

It's the great home newspaper of all this region :: It's the one recognized medium of advertising :: :: ::

Correspondence Solicited

E. B. MANN
UNDERTAKING COMPANY

311-313 CHURCH STREET
Old Phone 163   New Phone 144

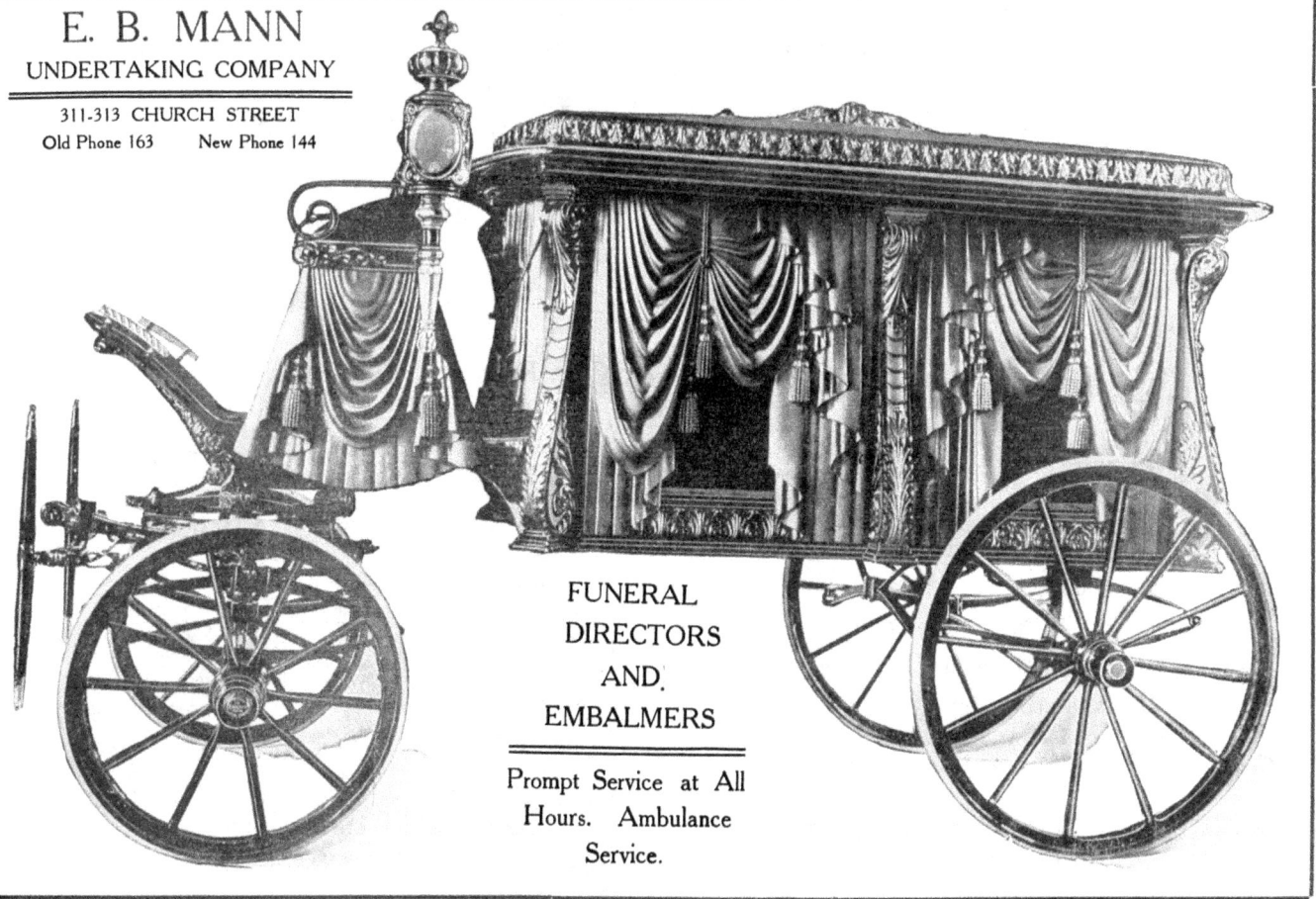

FUNERAL DIRECTORS AND EMBALMERS

Prompt Service at All Hours. Ambulance Service.

Alex McMillan

307 W. Clinch Ave.

REAL ...ESTATE

We are in position to suit any purchaser in a home or investment. Our facilities for selling property make it wise for any one owning property and wishing to sell to place their property with us.

We have salesmen who do nothing else but sell.

LOANS

We make loans on Knoxville improved real estate in amounts of $100 and up. We have made more mortgage loans in this city than all other mortgage loan agencies combined.

We write fire and plate glass insurance in best companies.

If you wish to rent a house, call and see our list. If you have a house to rent list it with us. We will find tenants, collect rents and pay your taxes and look after repairs.

JNO. M. BROOKS   J. B. MALCOM

BROOKS & MALCOM

Fire Insurance and Real Estate

This firm does a general Fire Insurance Business, and represents only the best companies.

Its Real Estate Business embraces houses and lots in the suburbs, farms and country homes, mineral and timber lands in this and other states. . . .

OFFICE: No. 3 DEADERICK BLDG.
New Phone 1548

H. H. GALBRAITH   JOE J. GALBRAITH

Harry Galbraith & Co.

....Real Estate....

OFFICE: ROOM No. 302 EMPIRE BUILDING
KNOXVILLE, TENN.

B. H. SPRANKLE   F. A. McSPADDEN

SPRANKLE & McSPADDEN

Real Estate Bought, Sold and Exchanged
We make a Specialty of Collecting Rents

The above firm is engaged principally in the Real Estate business, handling a large number of farms, suburban tracts, houses and lots. Although the present firm was organized a short time ago they have already a large and increasing business. Mr. Sprankle has laid out and developed many suburban additions around Knoxville, mostly West and South. The new firm is taking up a great deal of business along this and other lines. They have farms ranging in price from $300 to the magnificent river farms on the Tennesse River at prices from $5 000 to $20,000.

It is their object to put all renting property placed in their hands in good condition, having several men for that purpose. This insures the owners a good class of tenants and they become permanent renters. The firm of Sprankle & McSpadden make loans for their patrons on absolutely good security, netting to them six per cent. interest; which is double the rate of interest paid by the Knoxville banks.

SPRANKLE & McSPADDEN,
422 Union Avenue

New Phone 70   Old Phone 801

Success in Business

DEPENDS LARGELY UPON PREPARATION.

TRAINED Heads, SKILLED Hands, ALWAYS IN Demand.

ALL THE Commercial BRANCHES—
Bookkeeping, Shorthand, Typewriting,
Telegraphy, — Railroad wires
To Each Student's Desk.

Knoxville Business College

——— WRITE DEPT. 7 FOR CATALOG. ———

New Phone 1698 and 905   Old Phone 1186

JAS. E. THOMPSON

COMMERCIAL PHOTOGRAPHER

310 W. Clinch Ave.

KNOXVILLE, — — TENNESSEE

With O. C. Wiley

Hope Bros., Jewelers

THE firm of Hope Brothers, the leading jewelers of Knoxville, was founded in 1868, and has more than kept pace with the growth of the city. While strictly up-to-date in every detail of its conduct, it is of that old-time stamp of business concern whose name is a synonym of integrity, and whose word is an absolute guarantee of quality. This store is one to which a stranger would be directed if he were to ask for the most reliable jewelry store of the city.

This store, at 519 Gay Street, is ideally located, being in the center of the busiest and best block on the principal business thoroughfare.

Probably not in the South can be found a more extensive and attractive selection of Jewelry, Watches, Tennessee Pearl Jewelry, Diamonds and other precious stones.

As is well known, it is also the gift store of Knoxville. This fact is recognized abroad as well as at home, as may be seen by the fact that Hope Brothers are exclusive agents in Knoxville for Rookwood Pottery, Libbey Cut Glass, Teco Pottery, Pickard Hand-Painted China, and other notable gift art wares, sold only through the higher grade shops throughout the country.

The Manufacturing and Repairing departments are also very complete, and in them the most skilled and experienced artisans are employed. The Engraving plant is constantly overrun with orders for Wedding Invitations, Visiting Cards, Stationery, and Announcements of every character.

The Optical department is an important one and deservedly enjoys an enviable reputation and a liberal patronage.

While located in Knoxville, this firm has patrons in every part of the South, and their mail order business is of large proportions. While retaining all their old friends, this firm continues to increase its circle of new patrons, which is, in every sense of the word, true business success.

The Acme Electric Company

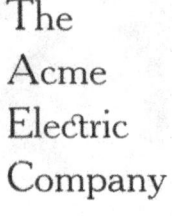

H. M. MOSES
PRESIDENT
AND
GENERAL
MANAGER

THE Acme Electric Company, Knoxville, was organized September 1, 1905, with H. M. Moses, president and general manager; F. S. Mead, vice-president; R. K. Gibson, secretary; L. P. Self, treasurer, and H. J. Henry, superintendent.

The company started business in a warehouse at 423 State Street, and moved to their present quarters, 702 Gay Street, January 1, 1906. They now occupy three floors and basement, having the largest stock in East Tennessee. They have just completed a fine fixture room on the second floor of their building, which will be used for display.

The Acme Electric Company does a larger business than any concern of its kind south of the Ohio River. This company has grown rapidly from the beginning. The company started with three wiremen and helpers, and now has twenty-five men constantly employed. They have installed several plants complete in East Tennessee and North Carolina, and have completed large contracts at Nashville and Louisville. Their motto is: "Satisfied customers bring more business," and their records show that their work always gives satisfaction and that more business follows completed contracts. The Acme Electric Company is prepared to figure on contracts of any size, and they make reasonable prices on all work.

BAIRD, CATES & CO.

... DEALERS IN ...

STOVES, FURNITURE and STOVE REPAIRS. . . . . .

AGENTS FOR GOOD WILL RANGES

TWO STORES---108 and 204 W. VINE AVENUE

EMPIRE AND DEADERICK OFFICE BUILDINGS

BAUMANN BROTHERS ARCHITECTS

OFFICES: SEVENTH FLOOR, HENSON BLDG.

KNOXVILLE, TENN.

MARKET HOUSE AND SQUARE

Something About Knoxville's Permanent Exposition of Good Things for the Table, and the Rich Section That Supplies Them

MARKET HOUSE

Knoxville may well be proud of her market. It is one of the greatest attractions for homeseekers to be found anywhere. Marketing is easy for the housekeeper, and a pleasure for each working day of the year where there are so many good things from which to make selections. Furthermore, it affords a ready sale for farm and garden products, and is therefore an attraction for all who wish to engage in farming, gardening or fruit growing. The small farmer and gardener looks first to the soil, then to opportunities offered for marketing the things he wishes to produce. Here he finds fertile soil, susceptible of the highest state of cultivation, and a market near at hand where his products may easily be disposed of at a good profit, either at wholesale or retail.

Small farms can be purchased at reasonable prices, situated on good macadamized roads within a few miles of the city. Intensive farming pays here. Large farms, within six or eight miles of the city, are being divided up, and in many cases each tract pays better with proper cultivation, than the whole body of land did under old methods.

We have referred particularly to the vegetable and fruit industries and the sections of the market in which

THE Knoxville Market House would be creditable to a much larger city. The display of vegetables, fruits, meats, fish, etc., that is made in its fifty-six well-arranged and well-kept stalls is not surpassed anywhere. In this big building is found an exposition of the products of field, farm, orchard and garden that are raised in one of the most fertile sections of the South. In addition to this, the wagons of truck farmers that stand in long rows all around Market Square are filled with the choicest varieties of all kinds of produce, for which there is always a ready sale. Visitors who go through the market house wonder at the great quantity of everything for the table that is exhibited on every hand—the wonder increases as they view the half mile of wagons packed closely on the sidewalks of the square, each one of which is a store in itself. The scene is not one that can be viewed in other Southern cities. Some have market houses and hucksters, but nothing that approaches what we have here.

INTERIOR VIEW OF NORTHERN PART OF MARKET HOUSE

MARKET SQUARE AT CHRISTMAS TIME

these products are sold. Something more should be said about meats. As fine beef cattle and hogs are raised in East Tennessee (the famous "Hay, Hog and Hominy" section of the South) as are found anywhere in the country, and the display brought from the abattoir and packing house of the city to the stalls of the market is not surpassed anywhere. Above all, cleanliness rules. The displays are appetising and pleasing. This is one of the main reasons for the great and growing business of the market.

Like all other sections of the Knoxville market, that devoted to fish and oysters is second to none in the South outside of coast towns. The best varieties of salt and fresh water fish are sold here, and they are handled in quantities to supply a large demand.

For ten years after the fish market was established the business paid little more than expenses. Since 1890 it has grown every year, the leading dealer now selling about 6,000 pounds of fish and 150 gallons of oysters weekly, while many others sell from 500 to 5,000 pounds each week.

J. A. BOWMAN & CO.
Wholesale, Retail,
and Shippers of
Fresh Fish, Oysters, Game and Poultry

WM. REED
Dealer in
FISH, OYSTERS and GAME

MATT WALTERS
Wholesale and Retail Dealer in Fine Celery, Strawberries, Fruits
Vegetables, Dressed Poultry, and Game in Season
43 City Market.   Old 'Phone 1629, New 'Phone 1106

W. H. GRAY
Dealer in Dressed Poultry, Butter, Eggs,
Fruits and Vegetables
GAME IN SEASON

PLEMONS & WARWICK
Dealers in
FRUIT, VEGETABLES, EGGS AND POULTRY
Game in Season

B. P. FLENNIKEN
Dealer in
Dressed Poultry, Butter, Eggs and Vegetables

J. A. BOWMAN & CO.
Wholesale, Retail,
and Shippers of
Fresh Fish, Oysters, Game and Poultry

WM. REED
Dealer in
FISH, OYSTERS and GAME

MATT WALTERS
Wholesale and Retail Dealer in Fine Celery, Strawberries, Fruits
Vegetables, Dressed Poultry, and Game in Season
43 City Market.   Old 'Phone 1629, New 'Phone 1106

W. H. GRAY
Dealer in Dressed Poultry, Butter, Eggs,
Fruits and Vegetables
GAME IN SEASON

PLEMONS & WARWICK
Dealers in
FRUIT, VEGETABLES, EGGS AND POULTRY
Game in Season

B. P. FLENNIKEN
Dealer in
Dressed Poultry, Butter, Eggs and Vegetables

The Knoxville Engraving Company

The Knoxville Engraving Co. started with a man and a boy on the top floor of 624 Gay Street six years ago. Each year the business has so increased that now as much work is turned out in one day as was at first done in a whole month. This company ships Photo-Engravings all over the United States from Maine to California, the orders being secured by sending samples through the mail to 35,000 people using Illustrations. The half-tones are made from photographs furnished by their customers or drawings they are prepared to make.

SALES DEPARTMENT
Where samples of work are shown and customers waited on.

PHOTO-ENGRAVINGS
AND
ZINC ETCHINGS
MADE FOR
ALL KINDS OF WORK

FINE COMMERCIAL
AND
CATALOGUE PRINTING
NEATLY AND
PROMPTLY EXECUTED

OUR NEW BUILDING
Four floors—60 x 100 feet. Run both day and night

CORRESPONDENCE DEPARTMENT
Here the mail orders are handled and letters answered.

The Knoxville Printing & Box Company

The Knoxville Printing & Box Co. occupies the same office and also do a large mail order business. Two years ago this company added printing, installing two presses. This was soon increased to four, and later to seven—two cylinders and five job presses. Eighteen months ago they moved with the Engraving Company into a four-story building 60x100 feet. In six months this was too small. They then ran a double shift, working a night and day force. This helped out awhile. Six months ago a part of the building next door had to be leased in order to take care of the increase in printing. We think this speaks well for the progressiveness of two of Knoxville's business institutions, who successfully meet competitors all over the United States.

www.ingramcontent.com/pod-product-compliance
Lightning Source LLC
Chambersburg PA
CBHW080347170426
43194CB00014B/2713